The
ECONOMIC DEVELOPMENT of
WESTERN EUROPE

The
Middle Ages
and the
Renaissance

Warren C. Scoville
J. Clayburn La Force

UNIVERSITY OF CALIFORNIA, LOS ANGELES

D. C. HEATH AND COMPANY
A Division of Raytheon Education Company
Lexington, Massachusetts

To
all those scholars of European economic history
who have made this volume possible

Cover drawings by Chester Okuniewicz

Preface

With this volume, along with four others in the series, we hope to provide supplementary readings for a range of courses in European history and the nucleus for a course in European economic history. Rather than composing a traditional type of text with its voluminous detailing of changing events, we have brought together a series of original studies on specific subjects written by eminent economic historians over the past four or five decades. We believe all of the essays to be significant contributions, many to be controversial, some to represent reinterpretations of traditional viewpoints, and all to possess a quality that will fire the interest of students and form a foundation for provocative discussions.

Prefacing this volume is an editorial essay designed to lay out very briefly and in broad strokes the economic characteristics of the period. Into this background each selected work takes its place and illustrates in detail and depth an aspect of Europe's economic history. A short, suggestive bibliography follows each article and guides the student to additional reading that at times offers a diametrically opposed view, a wider or perhaps a narrower treatment, a more general overview of the subject, or a diversion to some peripheral topic.

We have attempted to be discriminating in making our choices. One criterion was that as many of the selections as possible should be widely recognized as classics in the literature of economic history. Furthermore, we wished them to be broad enough in scope so that, when taken together, they would illuminate some considerable portion of Europe's economic history. We searched assiduously for contributions that possessed a rare combination of literary excellence, original research, and precise historical and economic analysis. Another important criterion hedging our judgments was the appropriateness of the study for undergraduate students. On the one hand, we endeavored to avoid highly complex, technical treatments, and, on the other, we sought to shun pedestrian, uninspiring research.

Since this is primarily a collection of readings, it leaves many aspects of the period untouched. Nevertheless, we believe it more fruitful to confront the student with a selective array of challenging and original works of prominent scholars than to provide him with a chronicle through which he drifts over a wide range of topics which may be superficially and summarily presented. It has been our desire to offer the professor an anthology which is amenable to different uses. For their courses in European economic history, some teachers who prefer informal methods of instruction may wish to employ this volume, along with the other four in the series, as the core for class discussions and to assign some of the suggested readings to individual students for a different point of view; other teachers may wish to assign the articles to their class and then in their own lectures to integrate, criticize, and elaborate on the readings; and still others may prefer to organize their lectures quite independently of any text and to leave it to their students to become familiar with important essays in economic history which might be inaccessible to them if the class is large and if the campus library resources are small. For courses in European history, instructors may wish to employ this or, as may be appropriate for specific courses, one or more of the other four volumes as supplementary readings or as the basis for class discussion.

We are indebted to the authors and their publishers for permission to reprint the essays we have selected. We wish especially to thank the Economic History Society for giving us permission to include articles which first appeared in *The Economic History Review*, some of which have subsequently been reprinted in volumes 1-3 of *Essays in Economic History*, edited by Professor E. M. Carus-Wilson, and published by Edward Arnold (Publishers), Ltd.

W.C.S.

J.C.L.

Contents

THE ECONOMIC DEVELOPMENT OF WESTERN EUROPE

Introduction

Though unmistakable omens were fortelling its ruin, the Roman Empire at the end of the third century A.D. was still a Mediterranean commonwealth with a widespread, closely interrelated commercial system, uniting Egypt, Syria, Africa, Spain, Gaul, and Italy. Most active was the eastern end of the Mediterranean, where Syrian merchants predominated. Into the highly developed, still rich Roman society stormed the Barbarians in the fourth century, intent on settling down en masse. Driven out and held at bay, these Germanic tribes grew stronger in number and military might until at the beginning of the fifth century they finally overwhelmed the badly weakened Romans, occupied all of the Mediterranean countries, and thus shattered forever the Roman hegemony.

The course of Western Europe's economic history from this triumph of Barbarism to the eve of a great commercial renaissance in the eleventh century is a subject of controversy among historians. In discussing the transformation of the West during these centuries, scholars have denoted the years A.D. 500 to 750 as the Merovingian Era, or the First Frankish Dynasty, and the years A.D. 751 to 987 as the Carolingian Era, or the Second Frankish Dynasty.

Some historians hold that the Merovingian and Carolingian epochs constituted one extended period of profound, unbroken commercial decrepitude, inaugurated by the destruction of the Roman Empire and its replacement by independent Barbarian kingdoms. Others contend that the Germanic tribes had developed a significant amount of civilization, including important economic methods and practices, before they had defeated Rome. And their conquest of the Mediterranean basin did not provoke nearly the havoc that historians once had thought.

Many characteristics of Roman society, including cities, trade, and contact with the East, therefore carried over into the Merovingian Age. Furthermore, these chroniclers believe that the Merovingian Era merged with Carolingian times and the later rapid expansion of commerce. Still another side of the debate accepts the concept of continu-

1

ity between the Roman and Merovingian epochs but then suggests that a sharp break occurred with the eighth century and the sweeping victory of Islam in the Mediterranean region and the subsequent raiding and conquering of the Norsemen in Northern Europe.

These two catastrophic events at the southern and northern peripheries of Europe abruptly severed the economic continuity from ancient times, and the economy of Carolingian Europe withdrew from the Mediterranean Sea, ceased to be one of towns and trade, and evolved instead into a tableau of large, independent agricultural estates—"an economy of no markets."

Persuasive, albeit sparse, evidence now prevails upon us to strike a middle course in interpreting how Europe's economy fared from A.D. 500 to 1000. While the magnitude of early medieval trade was never very large in absolute terms, testimony in the form of coins shows that trade at no time declined into insignificance. The same evidence also suggests that commerce failed to recover from the crisis of the Barbarian invasions in the fifth century. Coins of both silver and gold circulated in all Barbarian Europe, though in denominations smaller than those previously used by Romans. Between A.D. 700 and 850 rulers in Western Europe shifted to silver. Even Islamic Spain stopped minting gold coins. The silver *libra* replaced the gold *solidus* as the money of account, and silver pennies were the only Western money in circulation. At the same time, however, gold coins minted in the East and equivalent to the gold *solidus* were also current in Italy, Southern France, and the Spanish Levant. While the shift from gold to silver coins and the minting of smaller denominations in the West hints at a reduction of commercial activity, the concurrent circulation of gold coins from the East strongly insinuates that trade remained robust enough for merchants to use gold coins of large denominations.

Even though historical sources are woefully inadequate, we are able to sketch in broad strokes an outline of the composition of long-distance commerce during the Merovingian and Carolingian epochs. For it to have existed at all, there must have been professional merchants with capital, as well as some regions where specialization in production occurred. We know from contemporary sources that all products imported from the Orient in the fifth century still entered the West during the Merovingian and Carolingian eras. Perhaps the one exception was papyrus, for Western consumers had substituted the cheaper parchment for the more expensive papyrus.

From the fifth to the tenth centuries, and of course later on, markets in the West sold oriental silks and purple textiles, among other rare and luxury commodities. Spices graced the table of French noblemen all during these centuries. Even commerce with Islam was common-

2

place, as European merchants imported olive oils into Italy and exported slaves, iron, and timber to Moslem countries. On balance early medieval commerce was small in magnitude but highly complex.

Whatever might have been the precise nature of long-distance trade in the early Middle Ages, by far the dominant form of economic organization was the manorial, or seigneurial, system. Great estates universally characterized the scene of feudal Europe. Small farmsteads owned and operated by free peasants scarcely existed, and as centuries passed still fewer were to be found.

At the head of the great landed estate stood the seigneur, or lord, of the manor. Far more than the owner of the land, he was at the same time judge, protector, and chief of all those who lived on his property. Despite his position of seemingly supreme power, the lord's hold on his men fell short of complete ownership. Peasants were not human livestock. They cultivated fields on their own account, passed their lands from father to son, lived on part of the produce they created, and sold or exchanged some of it if they wished. Jointly, and in the common interest, they administered the arable land of the community and exercised customary rights over common pasture lands and waste lands.

The lord's ubiquitous prerogatives hedged the peasant's life at every juncture. Even though they held customary and heritable rights over land they tilled, peasants did not own the property. The same is true with grounds over which they exercised collective rights. The lord held a superior right over all land on the manor. Moreover, to their seigneur peasants owed in the first instance an important part of their time in the form of days of labor. They were expected to work in his fields, meadows, orchards, and vineyards, to haul his produce or materials and to build his barns and fences. Besides these burdens of time and effort, custom demanded that serfs provide their lord with a substantial portion of their products either in kind or in money.

Not only was the lord of the manor a renter of land and a beneficiary of labor services, but he was also something far more. The seigneurie was a unit of authority in which the power of the lord influenced all aspects of his peasants' lives. A customary law, administered by the seigneur or his agent, carefully set forth the relationship of people within the manorial community.

Besides those rules regarding landholding and services, feudal law bound each member of the community to the manor. No peasant could migrate from the village or permit any of his children to marry a person from another manor before gaining the lord's consent and paying the fines of *chevage* and *merchet*. When holdings passed from father to eldest son, the new holder had to give his lord the "best article of clothing," a tax assigned in the name of *heriot*. The obligation to pay *chevage, merchet,* and *heriot,* as well as a host of other dues and obligations, underlined the servile position of the peasants.

The estate itself possessed a village with a parish church, a manor house, and small, humble peasant dwellings put together of mud or wood and topped with thatched roofs. A small garden plot lay behind each peasant's hut and provided the family with vegetable gardens and chicken plots. Radiating from the village were, in succession, large cultivated fields, expanses of untilled pasture lands, and finally waste lands covered with scrub growth or forests. Perhaps a stream, with a meadow and swamp grass, traversed the manor. Astride this stream sat a mill for grinding the community's grain.

Although the most important source of food came from open fields and small garden plots, peasants of the community had valuable users' rights over the common pasture and waste lands. On these divisions of the manor serfs could keep bees, chickens, and geese, and pasture limited numbers of animals on common lands, as well as on stubble of harvested fields. When the lord acquiesced, peasants caught fish in his stream and hunted game in his foeests. Wood from the latter also supplied households with a strictly limited amount of fuel and building materials.

As this description of the manorial system has implied, a substantial amount of self-sufficiency marked each community, especially in the ninth and tenth centuries. Surely trade between great estates took place where peasants and lords exchanged some of their products for other commodities. By and large, however, the substantial part of all goods and services consumed came from the lands and workshops of the manor: cloth from the looms of peasants, tools from the lord's blacksmith shop, flour from his mill, bread from his oven, juice for wine from his wine press, and so forth.

Of central importance to the economy of the manor were the large arable fields, for from the harvests came the peasants' main supply of food. The community divided each field into parcels, or cultures, of eight or more acres. A further subdivision cut each culture into long, narrow strips. Enclosing about an acre apiece, each strip supposedly was of such an extent that a peasant with team and plow could till it in a day. Furthermore, it was narrow and long—perhaps two-hundred yards—to obviate frequent turnings of team and plow; at the end of each were "headlongs," or patches of land for reversing direction of the equipment. Balks, untilled ribbons of land, might separate strips from one another.

Oftentimes one field might contain fifteen cultures or perhaps many more, each one set to the contours of the land. Normally a peasant would hold anywhere from ten to forty strips in many different cul-

4

tures with no two strips adjoining. Instead of plowing, sowing, cultivating, and harvesting these strips independently, the peasants co-ordinated their efforts so that each large field, with its cultures and many strips, became one unit of production, on which they plowed their strips in unison, sowed the same crop, cultivated together, and co-actively reaped the crop when it had grown to maturity.

It was the introduction of the heavy wheeled plow, with its colter, horizontal share, and moldboard that led much of Europe, particularly the North, into this form of co-operative, large-scale agriculture. Because of the plow's weight and drag, peasants pooled their oxen and worked their fields jointly.

While the wheeled plow tied the activities of farmers together so intimately, it also led to a greatly increased output per man by making possible the effective tillage of fertile, but dense, river alluvia in Northern Europe. Furthermore, with the introduction of this new device, cross-plowing became needless, thereby adding even more to the productivity of peasants and leading to the system of strip farming. Previous to the plow's innovation and diffusion sometime before the eighth century, Northern Europe, with its deep, rich, thick soils, remained relatively undeveloped, in contrast to the south where the block system, cross-plowing, and the light Mediterranean plow predominated.

While the productivity of agricultural activity felt the beneficence of the fully developed heavy plow, even greater gains were to flow from the innovation of the three-field system late in the eighth century. By this method, arable land became separated into three large parcels. One lay fallow each year, one produced wheat or rye, and one grew another crop, perhaps peas or oats or barley. The following year peasants rotated the crops, maybe resting the field on which wheat had grown, sowing wheat where previously peas, oats or barley had grown, and planting peas or some other crop on the fallow field. Over a three-year cycle, each field had a year of rest, one devoted to wheat, and a third to peas or some other crop.

A significant increase in labor's productivity resulted whenever landowners switched from the two-field (in which one-half the land lay fallow) to the three-field system. For the adoption of the latter method meant an immediate increase of more than 30 per cent in currently productive land. And this occurred with an absolute decrease in acres plowed because each fallow acre received two plowings a year to thwart the inroads of weeds, and with the three-field system there were fewer fallow acres. Only in Northern Europe did this novel technique find widespread acceptance. Since the successful adoption of the three-field method required spring sowing and ample summer rains, landowners in the arid south did not find the new system profitable.

5

It is not mere coincidence but rather the legacy of this innovation that from A.D. 800 the agrarian economy of Northern Europe grew rapidly as compared to that of its counterpart to the south. Additional and perhaps even more striking boosts in agricultural productivity appeared in the late ninth or early tenth century with the innovation and diffusion of three more technological changes. These were the modern horse-collar, the tandem harness, and the horseshoe. The horse-collar afforded an increase of about 400 per cent in the pulling power of a given team, the tandem harness permitted the use of an indefinite number of animals in moving items of huge weight, and the horseshoe greatly increased this animal's efficiency by increasing its traction and reducing damage to its hoofs. Immediately the horse became far more productive, eclipsing the efficiency of the ox and giving man a significant increase in the nonhuman power at his command.

Yet the substitution of horses for oxen, like the substitution of three fields for two fields, occurred mainly on the northern plains. It was the earlier gains in productivity per man, a legacy of the heavy wheeled plow and the three-field technique, that allowed peasants to adopt the more expensive, grain-eating horse as a major source of power, while in southern climes the less productive two-field system condemned peasants to the retention of the cheaper, hay-eating ox.

As briefly sketched here, the manorial system had achieved its full form by the tenth century. The exact process that brought it to this point of development remains somewhat obscure. Subsequent changes, which were to alter the very economic foundations of Europe, appear in contrast far clearer.

Sometime around A.D. 1000 alterations in Europe's agrarian landscape appeared and with the passing of time they spread, widened, and deepened. Nevertheless, not all traditional ways and means collapsed at once, nor did modifications take the same form in all countries or within regions in any one country. In the eleventh century the transition appears first near places which were emerging as commercial centers.

Not until the fifteenth century, or even later, did some isolated districts far from major arteries of activity shuck off their feudal arrangements, while unmistakable remnants of Charlemagne's age lingered into the eighteenth century, standing out in harsh contrast and deep opposition to newer institutions.

Paradoxically, it may very well have been that the revolutionary success of feudal agriculture in the tenth century was in fact the catalyst of forces that destroyed that system itself. The heavy wheeled plow, the three-field system, the horse-collar, the tandem harness, and the horseshoe had been in succession diffused across Northern

Europe by the end of the tenth century, and subsequent to the substantial increase in output of food per peasant, population appears to have begun a remarkably swift ascent in the late tenth or early eleventh century.

Natural limits to the number of Europe's inhabitants had been lifted. The burgeoning population spilled out of the existing estates, emigrated to new ones formed at the expense of waste lands, repopulated towns and cities, joined the mercenary armies of princes, and became vagabonds, day-laborers, or merchants. The effect of the larger, more dense, and mobile population was to unleash forces that transformed the Western economy from one of large, independent agricultural units into one where cities and countryside, regions and nations joined in refined commercial and industrial relationships marked by a significant amount of specialization in production and exchange. From the productivity of this intensifying, widening specialization and exchange came much of the wealth that created the rich civilization of late medieval Europe.

As one of the initial consequences of the rising population, Western Europe witnessed large-scale projects of land reclamation and a consequent first breach in class and property relationships. Flemish people began to reclaim land from the sea by the start of the eleventh century, or perhaps as early as the tenth. Like projects first attacked the forests of Normandy and Maine at about the same time. The real "age of reclamation" occurred in France during the twelfth and thirteenth centuries, and the twelfth century also saw similar activity in Germany.

Religious houses such as the older Benedictine monasteries and new monastic orders like the Cistercians became heavily involved in clearing land. Some ecclesiastic and lay princes also joined in. These proprietors frequently engaged real clearance contractors who directed the task of reclamation. So sophisticated did this process become in some areas that wholesale clearers accepted orders and then dealt with subcontractors. The physical effort required to clear the land was supplied in part by peasants of the surrounding area.

Most important, however, were the foreign workers or colonists, who migrated from their native manors to these newer regions, lured there by promises of favorable conditions of tenure, personal status, and seigneurial rights. Called *hôtes* or "guests," they became a privileged class in the midst of the servile world of peasants. Although they did not gain title to the land, they usually obtained a hereditary lease with a small rent in money or kind and, unlike their compatriots on old cultivated lands, they normally owed no personal services. The *hôte* became a free man, for him the servile *heriot, chevage,* and *merchet* did not exist and his limited obligations were clearly described.

Grouped together in new agricultural villages or *villes neuves*, these people clearly constituted an important break with the feudatory conditions of most peasant communities.

Only a portion of the increasing numbers migrated to these *villes neuves*. Many others settled in growing urban centers and became professional traders or craftsmen. Coincidentally, the rural and urban populations entered into reciprocal economic relationships. The countryside renounced its self-sufficiency and turned to specializing in foodstuffs, which it then exchanged for items manufactured by city artisans, whose skills were sharpened by careful training, by the competition of their compatriots, and by the dedication to a single activity.

Urban craftsmen in their turn held a comparative advantage over peasant industry, their production efforts nurtured by city walls, municipal authority and services, and the wealth and knowledge of merchants. Here is the classic example of increasing returns emanating from a larger, more dense population. By virtue of its superior quality and relative cheapness, urban merchandise prevailed over peasant handicraft. In turn, entire agricultural regions commenced to concentrate their efforts along lines where their comparative advantages lay and then exchanged these specialties for those of other regions.

As the activities of cities, countryside, and regions thus merged into more intimate association, the old seigneurial arrangements disintegrated. For local and regional specialization to have progressed as it did, the entrenched users' rights of feudal origin first had to give way. The privileges that peasants held over the common and waste lands and the rights they exercised over arable fields had assured a self-sufficiency and a rigidly fixed pattern of resource use for the manorial society.

But from the eleventh century onwards, the self-sufficiency of large estates and the time-honored mode of using land yielded to rural specialization and with them necessarily went many feudal rights and privileges.

It clearly was to the advantage of the landowner to secure control over all his estate, for only then could he guide his lands into the newer, more specialized and thus more profitable employments. He not only sought control over his land but he also attempted to negotiate more flexible terms of tenure with his tenants.

When the eleventh century began, most seigneurs were receiving rents in kind or in money and personal services, all fixed in amount by centuries of custom. This meant that the proportion of income from the manor's fields received by the proprietor fell during the inflations that characterized much of the later Middle Ages. In effect, rising prices, leagued with the fixed terms of tenure, were transferring wealth from seigneurs to serfs. Only by substituting flexible terms for customary ones could landowners stop this.

The pattern of these adjustments varied from region to region. Usually landlords either took rents from their whole estate or cultivated the entire property. By the former method they rented their demesne and any other arable land they controlled. By the latter process they evicted customary tenants, added the land to their demesne, and managed the whole estate. Those who chose the last adaptation succeeded best of all, as illustrated by English lords. Yet, not all seigneurs fared well. Many faced severe hardships or even bankruptcy, especially those whose dues under the feudal system were inalterably fixed.

As these changes occurred, some peasants likewise suffered misfortune, especially those who lost their holdings to a seigneur who sought to manage his whole estate. But on balance most peasants gained. They benefited from having an expanded range of opportunities for employment in cities as merchants or free artisans and in *villes neuves* as non-servile tenants. The availability of these alternatives, plus the changing patterns of land use on older manors, enabled peasants to secure less restrictive terms of tenure in place of the older, servile ones. Greater independence, generally, and enlarged freedom in their economic activities, specifically, were thus their gains. Some peasants, especially in England, received the commutation of dues in kind and personal services in return for money payments. While personal services had amounted to about 120 days in Carolingian times, they fell perhaps to about twenty in the late Middle Ages.

In those regions where leases superseded customary tenures with their dues and services, the once complex personal bond between tenant and proprietor dissolved into a yearly cash payment as in England, or a fixed share of the crop as in France. Along with this change, hereditary tenures frequently evolved, and the land, in a very real sense, became peasant property, though burdened with perpetual and irrevocable dues. But now peasants could sell all or part of their land or buy additional portions. It was this significant fact that broke down the old standard holdings of unchangeable portions and substituted inequality in size of holding with the concomitant social distinctions based on property rather than birth.

Thus it was that feudal agriculture changed. No less striking alterations transformed the limits, character, and magnitude of long-distance commerce. Yet, as with the manorial system, these were not swift or uniform developments. Some regions remained untouched or felt the impact only partially or superficially; everywhere the countryside lagged behind the city; and in commercial and financial methods, Europe's southern regions preceded the northern by at least two centuries.

It was Southern Europe that witnessed the genesis of commercial revival, with Venice serving as the initial focus. That city's first inhabitants had chosen the inhospitable islets at and near Rialto as a refuge from the Barbarian invasion, and in order to survive they turned to fishing, salt preparation, and trade. Neither the Barbarians nor the Germanic emperors succeeded in dominating the Venetians, and since Italy had belonged to the Byzantine Empire when Venice came into being, that city remained a faraway outpost of Constantinople.

By the eighth century her merchants had risen to become the major provisioners of Constantinople, and her naval and mercantile power ascended dramatically during the following centuries. The first years of the eleventh century saw Venice, by virtue of her diplomatic acumen and naval might, become dominant among intermediaries of East and West. She maintained diplomatic relations with all Moslem countries and dealt as an equal with the kings of Italy and the Western Emperors. While her traders enjoyed full privileges of Byzantine citizenship, Venice mirrored the practice of Constantinople by taking under suzerainty several Istrian and Dalmatian cities and granting their merchants privileges in Venice.

Other Italian cities, notably Genoa and Pisa, at the end of the tenth century began to recover from about three hundred years of decadence, responding to the opulence of Venice and to the expanding opportunities for trade in the Mediterranean. It was the Catholic counteroffensive against Islam in the eleventh century, culminating with the Crusades, that brought Genoa and Pisa to commercial greatness. Early in the eleventh century they moved against and defeated Moslem forces on Corsica and Sardinia; thereafter they expanded their military adventures to the entire Mediterranean.

By the end of the eleventh century, Italians, now joined by other Catholic Mediterranean peoples, had reversed the previous conditions with Moslem and Byzantine countries. Western Christendom controlled the Mediterranean Sea once again.

The commercial activity of the Italian cities kept pace with their military ventures. By A.D. 1065 a Genoese commercial convoy had reached the Levant. Both Genoa and Pisa joined Venice in founding autonomous and permanent overseas settlements, thereby substituting continuous for intermittent trade between the eastern and western Mediterranean. Colonies appeared at Constantinople, Antioch, and Jerusalem before the Crusades, early in the eleventh century. Venice, Genoa, and Pisa built networks of trading posts around the Mediterranean shores. Other maritime centers of Italy, Southern France, and Catalonia imitated this example on a smaller scale, a process that reached its limits in the late thirteenth and early fourteenth centuries.

Religious scruples failed to deter Christians and Moslems from greatly expanding their mutually beneficial exchanges. From Islamic ports, Italians imported spices, perfumes, ivory, textiles, and oil, among other items, and in return they exchanged slaves, timber, iron, and wooden and metal goods.

The interests of Italian merchants in the Mediterranean naturally led them to travel with their wares to the nascent markets of Northern Europe. After the tenth century, the flow of goods moving north as well as south rose steadily. In the twelfth century, and especially in the thirteenth, the fairs of Champagne emerged as the locus for European merchants to meet and trade. Long before these fairs had lost their importance, Italian merchants and, in lesser numbers, other Mediterranean traders had settled in nearly every important city of Flanders, France, and England.

The character of northern trade differed widely from that in Southern Europe. Cruder, bulkier, more basic items, rather than the fabled, exquisite products of the Near East predominated. Only furs, a highly ranked item of Baltic trade, might be classified as a "luxury." Most important of all was food, for, as a direct consequence of regional specialization, places in the north such as parts of Germany, Scandinavia, Frisia, and in the later Middle Ages in Flanders, Brabant, and Holland, had begun to purchase agricultural products from afar. These foodstuffs, especially grain, came from the specializing areas of the upper Rhine and Northern France. Butter and cheese also entered foreign trade in significant quantities, provided by Holland, Scandinavia, Southern Poland, and even England. Perhaps of most importance was fish, a product of Scandinavian specialists, particularly of the Baltic fisheries of Skania off the south coast of Sweden.

Specialization went furthest of all in wine-making. Early in medieval times vineyards and the production of wine existed across Europe without any areas of emphasis, but beyond the eleventh century four major centers of wine production emerged—Poitou, Gascony, Burgundy, and the Moselle.

Of all raw materials, timber was the most prominent. An uneven distribution of timber resources characterized Europe, and forests were dwindling in size as population and cities grew. From the eleventh to the thirteenth centuries Scandinavia and Southern Germany were the main sources of timber exports; but in the fourteenth century, when Baltic trade opened, the coniferous forests of Russia, Poland, and Livonia became available, and soon timber from these regions predominated in foreign commerce. Pitch and tar also entered trade from these areas.

The principal manufacture was cloth. Using part of the wool which England exported in large quantities, Flanders developed an important textile industry. By the late fourteenth century, England and Holland entered the field and began to specialize in the production of woolens for export. Linen also became an important industrial commodity, especially for Flanders.

The initial centers of commerce and industry in the north were the feudal fiefs and baronies of the southwestern Low Countries. Early in the tenth century these regions came under the protection of the Count of Flanders, who formed them into a principality and achieved peace and order long before most other areas. From its geographical as well as its political attributes came the region's economic advantages.

Located on the North Sea, traversed in fortunate places by navigable rivers, possessed of sheltered estuaries for harbors from which its ships could comfortably pass to the sea, and blessed by an indigenous wool industry that provided wool for its weavers, Flanders readily expanded commercially and industrially. It was, perhaps, the only industrialized country in Northern Europe by the middle of the twelfth century. Ypres, Ghent, and Douai were centers of cloth production, and Bruges was the port city that served them.

While English, Flemish, and Italian merchants were most important in the eleventh century, Germans came to dominate northern trade by the thirteenth century. From Cologne the German influence spread. When the eleventh century opened, this German center was an important trade nucleus, with two fairs each year. A rich city, its wealth came partly from industry. Textiles and metal goods were the leading exports. But commerce provided most of Cologne's wealth. Her merchants became the middlemen between Central and Southern Europe on the one hand and Flanders on the other. The outer limits of German trade moved eastward from the end of the twelfth to the fourteenth centuries as the towns of Lübeck, Schwerin, Wismar, and Rostock, among others, expanded commercially, providing a new and cheaper access to Baltic timber, pitch, tar, furs, and other items. From this position of advantage, Germany became predominant in Scandinavia, developed much influence in Flanders, and obtained commercial privileges in England. When German towns combined into the Hanseatic League, a strong naval, military, political, and economic union of the fourteenth century, further expansion of trade to the east halted.

The vast changes in the magnitude, complexity, and geographical extent of Western Europe's economy took place in spite of a multitude and variety of impediments to the movement of merchandise. Formidable and innumerable fiscal exactions vexed traders at frontiers, along rivers, on roads, in seaports, and in town markets. And they grew ever more numerous as centuries passed. The Rhine River, for example, had nineteen tolls along its course at the end of the twelfth century, thirty-five or more at the end of the thirteenth, fifty at the end of the fourteenth, and in excess of sixty at the end of the fifteenth. Fortunately, merchants were frequently able to avoid the more heavily taxed routes by traveling alternative routes newly opened by treaty and agreement.

Whether journeying overland or by sea, merchants constantly faced the threat of piracy or warfare. Therefore, they moved together in groups seeking protection in numbers. Transport in any form was time consuming and costly in equipment and manpower. Most roads were dusty or muddy paths and necessitated the use of pack animals rather than carts to bear the major burden of cartage. Only where the state of roads permitted—and this was frequently only on the approaches to towns and rarely in the open country—did wheeled vehicles prove useful. Barges and boats provided the substitute par excellence for wheeled traffic. This was particularly true of England and Flanders, where numerous conveniently located, slow-moving rivers and streams afforded these regions natural avenues for moving goods.

To these many and varied obstacles to commerce must be added the uncertain consequences of the medieval views of economic life. Formulated and enforced by the Roman Catholic Church, these concepts held that each man performed a particular function in Society— ecclesiastics prayed, nobles fought and protected, peasants toiled. A man was not to attempt to raise himself above his natural position; he was to perform his appointed task throughout his lifetime, earning only enough to maintain himself in his rightful state, never seeking to amass wealth. Of all economic activities, trade was most damned, for here profits came not by the application of skilled hands to raw materials but merely by reselling already finished merchandise.

Perhaps the most vivid manifestation of these medieval views was the prohibition of usury, an interdiction against charges made purely for the use of money loaned or advanced. Unlike land, beasts of burden, or buildings, money was sterile. It could not by itself produce crops, power, or shelter, and thus should not be the source of interest. Besides, man should willingly help his needy brethren without any thought of gain. Exceptions did exist, and Church officials normally tried to enforce the prohibition of usury only when the lender took no risk and exacted a payment simply because he had made the loan.

Insofar as the maxims had any effect at all, they must have slowed and limited the mobility of labor, the spirit and nature of trade, and the evolution of financial procedures. Yet we must withhold too hasty a judgment as to the net effect. For in its role as an economic institution the Roman Catholic Church surely added something positive to Europe's material progress. The Papacy originated one of the earliest and most efficient financial systems of the Middle Ages. Its system of taxation, which embraced all of Western Europe and involved the gathering and transferring of relatively enormous sums, provided a fountainhead for the evolution of large-scale money and credit operations. To Italian banking houses, commissioned by the Papacy to serve as the Church's fiscal agents, fell the tasks of changing into currency of universal acceptance the diverse coins of local circulation received by ecclesiastical tax collectors, of depositing and transferring these monies, and of making loans to clergy who collected the taxes and frequently demanded advances. These activities subsidized and thus hastened the transalpine activities of Italian bankers, the growth in their numbers and financial strength, and the sophistication of their techniques.

The renaissance of trade in Europe came hand in hand with a robust resurgence of urban centers. In Roman times, the principal nuclei of population were the *civitates* or administrative centers of districts. Decline beset these urban concentrations after the final Barbarian invasions in the fifth century and proceeded at a faster rate in the north than the south. The Islamic eruption into the Mediterranean basin speeded up the process in the eighth century. Meanwhile, the ecclesiastic segment grew more important politically, socially, and economically. In the ninth century, the fall of the cities was almost complete. They had almost no free population of traders and craftsmen, and possessed no autonomy.

Another type of settlement took form from about the middle of the ninth century, when Norsemen threatened Northern Europe and royal authority dwindled. Local princes, assuming the task of defending the populations of their regions, constructed small fortifications called *castrum, castellum,* or burgs in strategic locations. Primarily centers of public and seigneurial administration with simple military populations, they possessed even less urban characteristics than the remnants of Roman towns. These burgs along with the Roman sites formed the cores around which cities and towns of the later Middle Ages were to germinate.

At the end of the Carolingian Era merchants began to settle in or around those ancient *civitates* and burgs that afforded convenient locations for their mercantile activities. The rebirth of urban centers occurred first in Italy, as well as along other coastal regions of the Mediterranean, and to the north along the Scheldt, Meuse, and Rhine rivers. The procedure of settlement varied widely. Some merchants and other immigrants settled within the old walls of ancient cities, while others settled outside the ramparts and constructed new ones for their protection. In many instances traders and artisans established themselves beneath the walls of the more recent burgs, encircling themselves in turn with defensive works. With the passing of time, the *faubourg*—the new enclosure—expanded many times and swallowed the primitive military enclosure. After the eleventh century, urban centers sprang up in much this fashion across the Continent. Parts of France in the twelfth and thirteenth centuries underwent an urban transformation, as Laon, Soissons, Rheims, Senlis, Noyon, Bayonne,

Bordeaux, and La Rochelle took on metropolitan characteristics. Towns in Germany also multiplied rapidly in the course of the twelfth and thirteenth centuries.

Merchants formed the active core of embryonic towns, and around these first immigrants soon gathered groups of artisans. Some of the latter produced items mainly for supplying the local population. In many centers a large segment of artisans, including those of numerous crafts, produced for faraway markets. Playing the role of entrepreneurs, merchants provided these craftsmen with raw materials and subsequently disposed of the finished output. By organizing mercantile and production activity, merchants acted as the indispensable propelling forces for the economic renaissance, particularly for the increased specialization and for the concentration of population in towns.

For these persons who settled in Europe's cities, there was no presumption of serfdom. Though of servile origin, a merchant or craftsman who came from afar and settled in the city was considered free. Authorities could not prove otherwise. Immigrants did not at first claim this freedom. As they came to recognize how advantageous it was for their mercantile interests they sought freedom as a normal condition for all townspeople. Authorities eventually agreed that by residing in a town for a year and a day a serf gained his freedom. In a corollary development, from the eleventh to the fourteenth centuries the towns themselves won their own political independence, becoming islands of autonomy in the midst of a feudal countryside.

As bases from which merchants sallied forth and as locations of specializing industrial activity, urban centers clearly were crucial to the economic resurgence of the late Middle Ages. But the enormous increase in long-distance trading between regions to the north and south and east and west owed perhaps an equal debt to the medieval fair. Set up in the open countryside rather than in cities, convened at stated intervals (normally once a year), and maintained anywhere from three days to six weeks, this institution became the center of international commerce in the eleventh century and thereafter for several hundred years. Merchants from all Europe gathered together at conveniently located fairs where they freely carried on the complex transactions of long-distance trade.

Early in their development fairs became endowed with many privileges and advantages. Provincial rulers excused traders from the normal taxes of the regions while the fairs held sway. Nor did princes apply feudal justice to activities related to the commercial congregations, but rather, a special merchants' law—a body of simple, speedy, and certain *ad hoc* rules—evolved as the basis for deciding disputes of all natures. Furthermore, officials of each fair regulated all details of the enterprise. They fixed the rents for booths and open space; they set moderate tolls and fees; they segregated the sellers of each commodity group to ease the task of buyers; at the larger fairs, they carefully set forth the timing of each event, permitting so many days for unpacking merchandise and a stated interval for the display and sale of textiles to be followed by similar periods for other items. Normally, near the end of each fair came a payment period when money changers and brokers took over the main scene of activity, extending credit to merchants, collecting debts outstanding from other fairs, and exchanging coins of different regions.

The pre-eminent fairs of Europe were those of Champagne in Northern France. Still small agricultural markets at the beginning of the twelfth century, they grew in importance as the region's population grew. A cycle of six fairs evolved in Champagne, providing a fair nearly the whole year around. On January 1, the fair at Lagny opened for an interval of six weeks; in mid-Lent the one at Bar-sur-Seine began a two-week term; that at Provins commenced on May 1 and was followed by one at Troyes on June 4, each for a six-week interlude. To end the year's cycle, Provins and Troyes each had another fair of six weeks beginning in September and October, respectively.

By the end of the twelfth century this sextet of fairs was truly the center stage of the Western World's long-distance commercial activity. To the plains of Champagne, which stood opportunely across the overland route from north to south, merchants from the four corners of Europe came to display their merchandise and to purchase the wares of others. The extensive movement of foreign exchange that inevitably arose from this concentrated foreign commerce brought into prominence money-changing activities. Thus it was that from the middle of the thirteenth century, the major emphasis of the Champagne fairs began to shift from mercantile to financial transactions. By the fourteenth century the primary function of most fairs had become the regulation of Europe's capital market.

Decline had beset the fairs of Champagne by the close of the thirteenth century. Competition of sea routes, dating from about 1320 onwards, lessened the geographical advantage that made Champagne the "turntable" for commerce between Northern and Southern Europe. Furthermore, Milan and Florence had by this time developed textile industries that both competed with the Flemish product and curtailed the prosperity of Italian merchants by reducing the market for northern textiles in the Mediterranean region. Another crucial factor that dimmed the importance of all fairs was the growth of urban centers, especially in Northern France and the Low Countries. With their harbors, warehouses, living accommodations, and other specialized services, large cities such as Bruges now offered advantages that lured into their precincts the conduct of the vastly more complex and expanded international trade of the early fourteenth century. Nevertheless, some fairs continued to operate throughout the fifteenth and sixteenth centuries, but their locations shifted from west to east, taking advantage of the contrast between the more industrialized West and the resource-producing East.

For nearly three hundred and fifty years Western Europe experienced a phenomenal economic resurgence. From a strictly agrarian system based on large, self-sufficient estates, an economy evolved where specialization reached untoward limits, and a marvelous apparatus of long-distance trade united the productive efforts of urban and rural regions as well as districts north, south, east, and west. Abruptly in the mid-fourteenth century, reversal set in, undoing much of the previous progress and leaving Western Europe in stagnation for over a century, from 1348 to perhaps 1465. Although the rate of descent varied from region to region, and the decline did not strike every region simultaneously, and while some places recovered temporarily, an overview of these darkened years reveals an undeniable cycle of regression.

In 1348 the Black Death ushered in the recession by killing perhaps as many as 25 to 33 per cent of the population of Western Europe, although a larger percentage of urban than of rural population. But since cities were the heart and soul of mercantile and manufacturing activity, the plague's ravages deeply wounded commerce and industry. This first terrifying blow was compounded by repeated appearances of plague throughout the fourteenth and fifteenth centuries. Germany suffered fourteen major visitations during the fifty years following the first appearance of the Black Death. Europe's population thus declined precipitously from 1348 until about 1400; thereafter it stagnated for a quarter of a century and finally began a slow recovery around 1425. Adding to the devastation wrought by plague, wars now lasted longer and became more destructive than they had been since the Norse invasions. France, the battlefield of the Hundred Years' War, suffered even more from armed conflict than from plague.

As war and plague within Western Europe did their damage to economic activity, so the shrinking of markets in the East added momentum to the decline of trade. Political disorders and wars in Asia, the expansion of the Ottoman Turks at the expense of Byzantium, and the more extensive abuse of Christian merchants by Egyptian sultans combined to reduce previous commercial activity with the East.

Convincing evidence clearly shows that the aggregate volume of Europe's industry and commerce suffered from these natural, political, and military calamities. For example, Flemish textile workers migrated in large numbers; Italian tyrants had to provide more extensive relief to the poor; 25 per cent of the inhabitants of Basle in 1425 lacked the minimum taxable capital of ten florins, and by 1453 this proportion had risen to 32 per cent; Florence had an experience similar to that of Basle; the proceeds of taxes in Marseilles declined; and the output of Florentine cloth dropped 50,000 pieces from 1338 to 1378. Moreover, data on international trade show that commerce at Marseilles from 1400 to 1480 was substantially less than it had been during the years 1250 to 1350. Similar data for England, Genoa, Dieppe, as well as for Marseilles, point to the years 1420 to 1465 as a time of decadence. In England and on the Continent agricultural output fell as did the extent of land under cultivation.

Despite the abrupt decline and lingering stagnation of aggregate economic activity, we must not too hastily infer that Europe's inhabitants were impoverished. To be sure, output fell, but so did population. Unfortunately, the current state of historical research fails to provide a satisfactory answer as to what happened to production per person. We can only make conjectures as to how certain segments of the population fared.

Many landowners most certainly lost, especially during the last half of the fourteenth century when population rapidly fell, for the declining supply of labor forced seigneurs either to pay higher wages or to accept lower rents. Peasants, the great bulk of the population, thereby gained. As their terms of employment or tenures thus became more advantageous, their falling numbers also led to the abandonment of less fertile or marginal land and a consequent rise in the output per man. Thus it was that rural wages rose and wheat prices fell.

How the urban population fared during the long recession is uncertain. The decline of commerce in Europe's major maritime ports probably exceeded 65 per cent over the years 1348 to 1465, a far greater drop than in urban population. Moreover, as population declined in the cities after 1348, urban industry experienced diminishing returns from the smaller, less dense population. Taken together, the large drop in the volume of commerce and the decreasing returns to industry most likely resulted in a decline in output per capita in urban centers.

The Place of the Netherlands in the Economic History of Mediaeval Europe*

Henri Pirenne

The place which the Netherlands[1] have occupied in the economic history of Europe is explained, like that which they have held in its political history, by their geographical position. Situated at the extremity of the "commercial axis" of France and also at the extremity of the great plain of Northern Germany, and fronting England along the whole length of their coasts, they form the meeting-place of the great lines of communication of the West. They are a place of junction and of crossroads, and if they have been the battlefield of Europe they have also been a peculiarly active centre of commercial attraction, while the convergence of transport routes upon them gave rise to an export industry from very early times. Whether viewed from the point of view of exchange or from that of production, their economic history exhibits a distinctly international character, and it is this feature, indeed, which gives it its unique interest.

I

Before the Roman conquest it was through the Netherlands that the tin imported from Britain took its way to the port of Marseilles.

* Reprinted from *The Economic History Review,* Vol. II (1929–30), by permission of the publisher.

[1] The word *Netherlands* is used in this article in its geographical and not its political sense—*i.e.,* to indicate the basins of the Scheldt, the Lower and Middle Meuse, and the Lower Rhine, which are now divided between France, Belgium and Holland.

On the other hand, the golden coins of the Belgian tribes, struck, like those of the Celts in Gaul, in imitation of the Macedonian staters, bear witness to the existence of relations between these tribes and the Mediterranean. The annexation of the country by Rome (57–51 B.C.) naturally introduced, together with security, the practices of a developed economic life. The soil was cleared and cultivated to a considerable extent, and the area cultivated seems to have remained unchanged from this period until the end of the eleventh century. Roads were constructed from the reign of Augustus onwards, and linked the whole region with the South; and by them it came in contact with Mediterranean civilization. There were, indeed, at this period, nothing but small provincial towns in the country which later was to become so decidedly urban. Tongres, Tournai, Bavai, Cassel were only secondary administrative centres, incapable of rivalling the towns on the banks of the Rhine and the Moselle. The population was mainly rural, but it lived in plenty. The excavations of the many villas discovered in Hainault, Brabant, Luxembourg and in the district of Namur have brought to light a style of furnishing which abounds in *objets d'art* of Italian or Oriental manufacture, and marble imported from Illyria and Africa was used in decoration. The raising of cattle was a considerable occupation, and the hams and geese of Belgium were the delight of Roman "gourmets"; while the sale of cereals was assured, thanks to the military administration which bought them for victualling the legions encamped along the Rhine. By the side of such purely agricultural pursuits there existed a rural industry which appears to have been particularly active. The brass manufacture was carried on on the banks of the Upper Meuse, while forges were plentiful between the Sambre and Meuse, and glass works around Namur. Pottery was made with such skill that its products can be acclaimed as the most perfect produced in any Roman province. Finally, in the plains by the coast, where the woollen industry was to flourish so greatly in the Middle Ages, cloaks *(sage)* and mantles *(birri)* were already being manufactured and exported to the other side of the Alps. All this evidence leads to the conclusion that Belgium, undoubtedly, owes the beginnings of her industrial life to Rome. Commerce was carried on both by land to Gaul and Italy, and by sea to Britain. Boulogne, where the routes from the Mediterranean met the sea, was an important traffic centre, and at Domburg, at the mouth of the Scheldt, the remains of a temple to the Celtic goddess Nehallenia, patron of navigation, have been discovered. The *Classis Germanica,* which had its workshops at Mayence, had established branches at Nimwegen, at Leyden, at Katwijk, and at Rumpst on the Rupel.[2]

---

[2] F. Cumont, *Comment la Belgique fut romanisée,* xxvi. (Brussels, 1914).

It is a very significant fact that the Frankish occupation of the Netherlands in the fifth century did not destroy this economic life. No doubt the troubles and the rapine inseparable from an invasion must have given it some serious shocks, but it is noticeable that its principal features reappear in Merovingian Gaul from the reign of Clovis. In spite of the scanty evidence, we know for certain that up to about the year 700 Mediterranean commerce was still spreading all kinds of Oriental spices over the country.[3] Papyrus, imported from Egypt, was so plentiful that it could be regularly bought at the market of Cambrai, and no doubt in many other places. Shipbuilding and seafaring must have retained their importance at Maestricht and at Duurstede near Utrecht; and so must the brass industry at Huy, to judge from the large number of coins struck in these districts in Merovingian times. It is certain also that the woollen weaving, which was so flourishing in the ninth century, cannot have disappeared in the course of the preceding centuries.

II

The serious crisis caused by the irruption of Islam into the Mediterranean basin, which coincides with the beginning of the Carolingian period, had an immediate repercussion in the Netherlands. Closing the Mediterranean along the coast of Gaul, and severing the relations of the latter with Syria and Egypt, it dried up the stream of commerce from Marseilles which had not ceased, even after the fall of the Roman Empire, to reach and vivify the districts of the north. From the reign of Charlemagne onwards clothes cease to be made of silk and the spices and wine of Gaza disappear from the list of foodstuffs. Just as the latter no longer includes anything but indigenous commodities, so none but linen or woollen garments are any longer worn. This alteration, imposed by external forces on the habits of the people, seems to have turned to the advantage of the woollen industry in which the ancestors of the Flemings had already been long engaged. It is certain that from the beginning of the ninth century this industry enjoyed an extraordinary popularity. It was the only one which was vigorous enough under the Carolingian Empire to carry on an export trade. The so-called Frisian cloths *(pallia fresonica)* mentioned in the writings of the period were undoubtedly woven in Flanders,[4] but, as

---

[3] H. Pirenne, "Un contraste économique, Mérovingiens et Carolingiens," in *Revue belge de philologie et d'histoire* (1923), 223 *seq.* See also *Mediæval Cities,* 18 *seq.* (Princeton, 1925).

[4] H. Pirenne, "Draps de Frise ou draps de Flandre," in *Vierteljahrschrift für Social und Wirtschaftsgeschichte* (1909), 308 *seq.*

often happens in commercial history, they have been named from the people who transported them, and it was in Frisian ships that they were carried from Duurstede and Utrecht down the valley of the Rhine. These cloths, made by the peasants on the coasts or by the women in the women's working houses (*gynecea*) of the great estates of the Scheldt basin, were not only beyond the reach of competition for their quantity, but also for their fineness and beauty of colour. It was Frisian cloth which Charlemagne chose to offer to the Caliph Haroun al Raschid in return for his gifts. It must be supposed that it was thanks to the preservation of Gallo-Roman technique, and in particular of the processes of fulling and dyeing, that the Flemish cloth industry from that time onwards exhibited all the characteristics of a luxury industry which it was to keep until the end of the Middle Ages. Its curious prosperity in this period is all the more remarkable because of the striking contrast which it forms with the essentially agricultural civilization to which the closing of the Mediterranean had reduced Western Europe. Except in Italy and in the Netherlands the economy of that period was a self-sufficing economy. It realized its classic form in the organization of the great estates after the type laid down in the *Capitulare de Villis*. In the absence of markets, none of them produced more than sufficient for the needs of their proprietors and of the *familia* of serfs who cultivated the ground, and in consequence each made a point of producing everything necessary to its own subsistence. In these conditions the circulation of money was reduced to the strictest minimum. Not only were silver coins substituted for gold from the reign of Charlemagne, but rents were almost always paid, and feudal dues of all sorts rendered in kind. Nothing is more certain than that the Netherlands were forced to adopt this retrogressive economy. The fact that nearly all the monasteries in this region, where the cultivation of the vine is impossible, made a point of obtaining estates in the vine-growing countries, either in the valleys of the Rhine and Moselle or in that of the Seine, as gifts from their benefactors, proves that they were unable to obtain wine by ordinary commercial means.[5] The privileged situation of the Netherlands prevented them, however, from being entirely confined to this marketless economic system. In spite of everything a certain commercial activity continued to manifest itself, not only among the Frisians at Duurstede and Utrecht, but also at Quentovic (Estaple) on the Canche, which was a very active port. The extent of the relations between these places and the North is most positively attested for us by the discovery of their coins in England and even on the shores of the Baltic. It is characteristic also that the

---

[5] H. van Werveke, "Comment les établissements religieux belges se procuraient-ils du vin au haut Moyen Age," in *Revue belge de philologie et d'histoire* (1923), 643 *seq*.

only gold coins minted by the Carolingian kings besides those of Uzès were struck in Friesland.[6] The influence of maritime commerce was naturally felt in the interior, and its repercussion developed river transport. *Portus,* that is to say depôts and staples, existed on the banks of the large rivers, and Tournai and Valenciennes on the Scheldt and Maestricht on the Meuse had become or had continued to be important agglomerations of merchants and shipbuilders. Thus, although the Netherlands had ceased to be the most distant point of focus for Mediterranean traffic as they had been during the Roman and Merovingian periods, yet, thanks to their woollen industry and to their commerce on the rivers and the North Sea, they still presented an aspect which could not be paralleled north of the Alps. If they had escaped the catastrophe which brought upon them the inroads of the Northmen in the second half of the ninth century, they might have gradually extended their commercial activity around them and have considerably hastened the economic renaissance of Western Europe.

The cause of the sudden descent of the Northmen on England and the Continent in the ninth century is still unknown. It is extremely probable that it may be considered from some points of view as a consequence of the invasion of Islam. What is known of the commercial relations which the Swedes maintained with Mohammedan Asia by way of the Volga and the Caspian Sea, as early as the eighth century, leads us to believe that they had considerably developed the navigation of the Baltic. Impelled by their example, the Danes and Norwegians in their turn set out on those expeditions of commerce and piracy which were naturally directed towards the British Isles and the shores of the continent facing the North Sea and the Atlantic. Whatever the truth may be, the disasters which they inflicted on these districts were immense. The Netherlands, which the large river estuaries laid widely open to the enemy fleets, suffered more from their ravages than any other country. All its monasteries and all its ports were pillaged or reduced to ashes. Quentovic disappeared: Duurstede was ravaged four times in succession. It was only after the victory won by Arnoul of Carinthia at Louvain in 891 that the barbarians ceased to attack a country which was by this time in a state of complete exhaustion and no longer offered them a sufficiently tempting spoil. It is needless to remark that during these years commerce and industry disappeared for the time being, but they were not slow in reviving. The geographical situation of the country was too favourable for their eclipse to last long, and they recovered after the Norman invasion of the ninth century just as they had done after the Frank invasion of the fifth century.

---

[6] M. Prou, *Les Monnaies carolingiennes,* xxxiii. (Paris, 1896).

III

It may even be asked if the Normans themselves did not contribute to the revival. Their invasions had only been the violent prelude to the period of maritime supremacy which they exercised in the North Sea and in the Baltic, before they were dispossessed in the twelfth century by the Teutonic Hansa. As soon as they began to substitute more peaceful pursuits for military activity, they appear as merchants along those rivers of the Netherlands which they had visited, in the first place, as pirates. It is known for certain that in the tenth century they were carrying on trade at Utrecht and in Flanders. It was probably through their agency that the coins struck in a number of places in the Netherlands began, from this time onwards, to penetrate into Sweden, to the isles of Götland and Öland and even as far as Poland.[7] The inhabitants of the country, for their part, soon began again to utilize the means of communication which nature had put so generously at their disposal. The inhabitants of the valley of the Meuse may be traced, descending the river to its junction with the Rhine, ascending the latter to Cologne and thence travelling to Goslar to provide themselves with the copper which they needed for the metal industry, now reviving at Huy and Dinant. On the other side of the country, on the coast of Flanders, commerce sprang up again between Bruges, which was beginning to grow at the base of the gulf of Zwin, and the Thames estuary. The market tariff of London (991–1002) mentions the merchandise sold there by the Flemings, and also names the men of Liège, Nivelles, and Huy.[8] It is almost certain that the latter came to buy the tin which they needed for their brass manufacture. As to the Flemings, no doubt they imported cloth and exported in return cargoes of that fine English wool which was soon to become the main raw material of their industry. The international character of economic life thus reappeared with its revival. The commerce which the Netherlands carried on with foreign countries, exporting the produce of the national industry and importing raw materials, presents a very different appearançe from the petty chaffering round a local market, which, according to a far too prevalent theory, preceded the economic revival of Europe. In reality, both in the Netherlands and in Italy, this revival was brought about by long-distance commerce.

---

[7] Al. Bugge, "Die Nordeuropäische Werkehrswege im frühen Mittelalter," *Vierteljahrschrift für Social und Wirtschaftsgeschichte* (1906), 227 *seq.*

[8] Liebermann, *Die Gesetze der Angelsachsen,* i., 232.

In the absence of exact information, the status of the travelling merchants and navigators of the tenth century admits only of hypothesis. There is nothing which would lead one to see in them the servants to whom certain monastic houses entrusted their provisioning, and who gradually emancipated themselves and carried on trade on their own account. The general arguments against this view are all the stronger in the case of the Netherlands because merchants acting for monastic houses are unknown there. Everything which can be gathered about the early *mercatores* of the Netherlands obliges us to consider them as independent of manorial power. From what class did they come? If that is a question which cannot be answered with certainty, all the evidence, at any rate, points to the fact that they must be looked for among those *vagantes,* those *pauperes,* in brief those vagabonds who, lacking land, wandered about society in search of a living. Some lived on alms, others took service in the army, others, no doubt, took the chances involved in entering upon the career of a wandering trader. They must be regarded as bold and enterprising adventurers. Capital they had none. Among them we cannot trace a single landowner selling his property to realize capital wherewith to enter trade. Very primitive forms of credit must have sufficed for their operations. Others may have been enabled by some lucky chance to build up a basis from which to start. But above all, and this is particularly important, they did not work singly. Nothing could have been less individualistic than their method of trade. It was only carried on thanks to the possibility of association, which multiplied the results of their efforts by uniting them. The merchant gilds, which appear as already solidly established in the eleventh century, must be as old as the revival of commerce; for this commerce, whether by land or sea, was a commerce of caravans. It was in armed bands, rigidly disciplined, headed by a chief (the *doyen*), and flying each its own flag that the *mercatores* appeared at the markets. Whether they called themselves gilds, hansas, or charitable associations (*caritas*), their aspect and object was always the same. As commercial activity became more intense they began to specialize. In the twelfth century all the Flemish groups which carried on trade in England were federated in a vast association bearing the name of the "Hansa of London."[9]

The territorial rulers were lavish of support to these merchants who, by paying the transit dues (*teloneum*) which were so frequently charged along the roads and rivers, contributed largely to their finances. They took them under their especial protection, and the laws which they promulgated inflicted punishments, even up to the death penalty,

---

[9] H. Pirenne, "La hanse flamande de Londres," in *Bullet. de l'Académie Royale de Belgique,* Classe des Lettres (1899), 65 *seq.*

for offences against these useful travellers. Further, the merchants had direct access to the royal court—*i.e.*, to public jurisdiction. The manor courts could not summon them; for the merchant, wherever he went, was treated as a freeman, though many were certainly the younger sons of serfs who had left their fathers' *mansus* to seek adventure. Who could tell outside the manor where they were born? Their wandering life wiped out all traces of their origin and no one knew their civil status, so that they had to be treated as freemen; for the status of serfdom could not be presumed. It must be noticed therefore, and it is an observation of the highest importance, that, from its very beginning, commerce developed under the régime of personal liberty.

It goes without saying that the wandering life of the merchants made indispensable a certain number of fixed posts around which they gravitated. Such a life could not dispense with permanent centres which could serve as winter quarters, as depôts for the collection of goods, and for shelter to ships and wagons. It is obvious, moreover, that the situation of these places must correspond to the needs of commerce—*i.e.*, that they must be fixed on those spots where the lie of the ground, the course and depth of the rivers, and the height of the banks naturally provided opportunities for passage and for an assemblage of people. Thus, in the course of the tenth century, concentrations of merchants grew up, for example, at Ghent at the junction of the Lys and the Scheldt, at Bruges at the base of the Zwin estuary, at Cambrai where the Scheldt ceases to be navigable, at St. Omer on the Aa, at Lille on the Deule, at Douai on the Scarpe, at Maestricht where the road from Cologne to the sea crossed the Meuse, at Liège at the junction of the Meuse and the Ourthe, and higher up the Meuse at Huy and at Dinant.[10] These collections of merchants have a characteristic name, that of *portus*—*i.e.*, ports, depôts, bases for merchandise. The name well indicates their essentially commercial character. It is the original of the Flemish word *poort* which means town, and, even if all the other evidence did not point in that direction, it would need nothing more to prove that the towns of the Netherlands owed their origin to commerce. While in France and on the banks of the Rhine and the Danube the revival of town life took place, almost without exception, in the ancient Roman cities, in the Netherlands, on the contrary, the oldest and most active centres are generally to be found in new towns. Only Tournai and Cambrai are earlier than the Middle Ages. Everywhere else the merchant group which formed the germ of the town is completely cut off from the ancient tradition.

---

[10] H. Pirenne, "Les villes flamandes avant le XIIe siècle," in *Annales de l'Est et du Nord* (1905), 9 *seq.* G. Des Marez, *Étude sur la propriété foncière dans les villes du Moyen-Age et spécialement en Flandre* (Gand, 1898).

But that was not because the towns were built on virgin soil. Wherever the *portus* grew up there was already a fortified enceinte, built after the invasions of the Northmen, to serve as a refuge for the people of the neighbourhood, and it was around the walls of these "burgs" that the merchants collected. But it would be quite incorrect to believe that the "burg" had given birth to the town. The town was in its immediate neighbourhood, but it did not develop out of it. The contrast between the two is as clear cut as possible, for the "burg" was intended for military purposes only; its garrison of knights lived on the revenues of the neighbouring soil, and its size remained stationary. The *portus,* on the contrary, lived only by commerce, and, growing in proportion as its increasing activity attracted newcomers, it soon surrounded the ancient feudal fortress with its new quarters, shut it in on all sides, and finally absorbed it. Even by the twelfth century this process had taken place. The now useless walls were demolished and turned into building land. The merchant *portus* had assimilated the feudal *burg* and finished by appropriating its name. Originally the merchant settlement was surrounded with a palisade which sheltered it from robbers, and soon this wooden defence gave way to a wall, always extending in size, built of solid stone ramparts edged with ditches. From thenceforth the *portus,* in the centre of which the old *burg* was falling to ruins, became itself the *burg*; and from the end of the eleventh century its inhabitants bore the new name of burgesses *(burgenses),* so that by a curious change of meaning the "bourgeoisie," born of commerce, are designated by a name borrowed from feudal language.[11]

IV

At the beginning of the twelfth century a new and external impulse affected the economic activity of the Netherlands. Just as the closing of the Mediterranean by Islam had put an end to their relations with the Southern countries, so these were renewed with the revival of navigation there by the Christian countries. The Netherlands became that meeting-place for the commerce of Italy and of the North which they were to remain until the end of the Middle Ages. Before 1127 Lombard merchants were attending the Flemish fairs, and it was their presence which gave these fairs, established at Thourout, Ypres, Messines, Lille and Douai, the importance of which the famous fairs

---

[11] What is said here of the part played by the *burgs* applies equally to the places where the *portus* of merchants attached itself to the fortified seat of an episcopal *civitas* as at Tournai, Cambrai and Liège.

of Champagne were to rob them in the thirteenth century. But the transformation of the latter into international centres of European commerce did nothing to diminish the intensity of the relations between Flanders and Italy. It rather benefited both by putting them in contact with the movement of European commerce of which they were the centre. The Italians came to Flanders to buy cloth for which payment was made by "fair letters" on the fairs of Champagne.[12] On their side the Flemings came to sell their stuffs at Troyes, at Provins, at Lagny and at Bar-sur-Aube, and this made them a more and more popular item in the general stream of commerce. The fairs of Champagne served the Flemish merchants at once as a clearing-house, if one may use such a word of that period, and as a new market for their trade.

The increase in economic activity in the twelfth century resulted in the creation of a considerable number of very rich men among the merchant class. We know, from the account of a certain Werimbold, given in the *Gesta episcoporum Cameracensium,* the way in which a large fortune was acquired, and the nature of capital investments. Werimbold, beginning with nothing, entered the service of a rich bourgeois and was given the superintendence of his business, met with marvellous success and ended by marrying his master's daughter. The gains which he made in commerce he invested in purchases of land and in urban rents, and thus became a great landed proprietor.[13] His story is that of many others. At the beginning of the thirteenth century, in fact, the land belonged entirely to a class of rich merchants, new men, to whom the texts give the characteristic name of *homines heredi-tarii.* Not all, moreover, limited themselves to investing their trade profits in real property. Many, like William Cade of St. Omer,[14] or Simon Saphir and Salomon Rinvisch of Ghent, or the Louchards of Arras, devoted themselves particularly to finance.[15] They lent considerable sums to the King of England, to the Count of Flanders, to feudal lords and to towns in search of loans. It was no doubt to obtain forgiveness for these transactions, which were entirely condemned by the Church under the name of usury, that they vied with each other in charitable foundations. Werimbold redeemed the duty which oppressed the citizens at one of the gates of Cambrai, others built hospitals for the sick, asylums for the aged and infirm, and so on.

---

[12] G. Des Marez, *La lettre de foire à Ypres au XIIIe siècle* (Brussels, 1901).

[13] *Gestes des évêques de Cambrai de 1092 à 1138,* ed. Ch. de Smedt, 122 *seq.* (Paris, 1880).

[14] H. Jenkinson, "William Cade," in *English Historical Review* (1913), 209 *seq.* Cf. *ibid.,* Vol. XXVIII, 522 and 730, and "A Moneylender's Bond of the Twelfth Century," in *Essays offered to Dr. Poole* (1927), 190 *seq.*

[15] G. Bigwood, "Le régime juridique et économique du commerce de l'argent dans la Belgique du Moyen Age," *in Mém. in 8vo de l'Acad. Royale de Belgique,* second series, Vol. XIV (1921).

Towards the middle of the thirteenth century the improved processes of exchange and credit which the Italians introduced into the Netherlands made it possible for the latter to take the place of the native financiers, and from that time onwards the capitalists of the country only meddled sporadically with finance, which was entirely annexed by the Italians, who were known in current language as Lombards or *Cahorsins,* though merchants of Cahors seem to have been exceedingly rare on the shores of the North Sea.

While Italian moneylenders abounded in Flanders and shortly afterwards in all other parts of the Netherlands, Jews, on the contrary, were very scarce. It is curious to notice that the more active, economically, a region showed itself the less the Jews appeared in it. They seem hardly to have taken part in business at all, and to have confined themselves exclusively to petty moneylending transactions. In 1261 the Duke of Brabant, Henri III., ordered their expulsion from the duchy in his will; but his widow, the Duchess Aleyde, did not carry out this measure, but consulted St. Thomas Aquinas about the proper treatment to apply to them.[16] In a word, the part they played was negligible. A case of sacrilege in 1370, in which a Jew was accused, brought about their expulsion from Brabant, and from that date they are hardly mentioned in the Netherlands. They only reappear under entirely different conditions, first at Antwerp and then at Amsterdam, in the course of the sixteenth century.

All that has been said above of the commercial movement proves how intimately it was linked with industry. No doubt it was not the latter which had called it into being, for the geographical situation of the district was bound to attract it; but it is none the less evident that the country's industrial life hastened its appearance and contributed largely to its progress. Thanks, no doubt, to the preservation of Roman technical methods, manufactures were, indeed, distinguished for their excellence. It has been seen above that this was the case with the cloth of Flanders, and the superiority of the brass goods made in the valley of the Meuse is attested by the introduction of the word *"dinanderie"* into commercial language. If the soil of Belgium produced no commodity such as wine or salt which compelled the foreigner to come and buy, this disadvantage was largely compensated by the products of her industry. Thanks to them she could even supply an export trade, the growth of which was increasingly accentuated from the tenth century onwards. We must notice, further, that the nature of the native industry made it necessary to import raw material from

---

[16] H. Pirenne, "La duchesse Aleyde de Brabant et le 'de Regimine Judaeorum de St. Thomas d'Aquin,'" in *Bull. de l'Acad. R. de Belgique,* Classe de Lettres (1928), 43 *seq.*

abroad. The country produced neither the tin nor the copper necessary for the metal-workers of Huy and Dinant, and they were forced to get them from Germany and England. The woollen industry, though probably it originally employed native wool, soon abandoned it for the finer and silkier English wool of which Flanders was the principal consumer to the end of the Middle Ages. Thus Belgium, as early as the twelfth century, exhibits the same characteristic features as mark her to-day—those of an industrial country dependent on foreign countries for her raw material, and for that very reason unable to maintain herself except by export.

The progress of industry had the further result of centralizing it in the towns. During the Roman period, as well as in Merovingian and Carolingian times, the woollen industry was carried on in the country, and in those days it was an occupation for women, relegated to the peasant's wife or to the female serfs (ancillae) of the manorial gyneceum. In proportion, however, as the demand for its products grew, production began to migrate towards the portus, where the merchants who bought it resided, and men took the place of women in the manufacture of cloth from the day when it became a specialized occupation. At the same time its technique was modified. The pieces had at first been only of the small size (pallia) suitable for making cloaks. It was found more practical to increase their length to facilitate packing and transport. The ordinary length of a piece of cloth is, even today, imposed by the demands of commerce, and, while we are not able to fix exactly the first appearance of this practice, it is extremely probable that it goes back to the twelfth century. At this period the concentration of the woollen industry in the towns was an accomplished fact. Outside them, only a few weavers survived in the flat country; and from the end of the twelfth century the continuance of even this slight competition was forbidden. Every town reserved for itself the monopoly of weaving and of all the complicated operations concerned with the manufacture of woollen goods. Only one of them, spinning, was carried on outside the walls. The urban clothiers gave out wool to the peasant women of the neighbouring country who returned it as yarn, and the female weavers of an earlier period are now transformed into spinners.

By the middle of the thirteenth century the Netherlands had acquired the appearance which they were to retain throughout the whole of their subsequent history. They had become par excellence a country of towns. Nowhere, north of the Alps, are towns so numerous, so rich or so active. In this respect the Flemish plain recalls the Lombard plain. The urban movement developed from two centres— one the basin of the Meuse, the other that of the Scheldt. In the first, as one descends the river, are Dinant, Huy, Namur and Liège, all engaged in the metal industry; then the commercial towns of Maestricht, Utrecht and Dordrecht. The second area, assisted by its situation on the seacoast, shows a denser agglomeration. Valenciennes, Cambrai, St. Omer, Lille, Douai, Ypres, Ghent and Bruges were, from the middle of the twelfth century, extraordinarily active centres, where commerce and the woollen industry developed together and reacted on each other. Between the district of the Meuse and that of the Scheldt relations were at first few and far between. The latter turned towards the sea, the former towards the Rhine and Germany. But in the course of the twelfth century the vigorous vitality of the Flemish area attracted the commerce of the districts bordering on the Meuse; its magnetism made itself felt as far as the Rhine, and all the commerce of the Netherlands converged more and more upon it, or, more properly speaking, upon the port of Bruges, the importance of which grew astonishingly in the course of the thirteenth century. Thanks to the commercial current from the Meuse to the sea, Brabant, situated between the two, revived, and in its turn became covered with towns.

About 1150, Antwerp, Malines, Brussels and particularly Louvain, began to compete with their older rivals in the East and West. At the same period secondary towns grew up, in increasing proximity to each other, round all the centres where urban life had first sprung up, along the roads and rivers which penetrated the country. They were so numerous in Flanders and in Brabant, that in the course of the thirteenth century the urban population may be said to have been as large and perhaps larger than the rural. What is quite certain is that in number of inhabitants the principal towns of these areas were not equalled by any elsewhere in Western Europe. Their growth was so rapid between 1100 and about 1350 that their walls had to be enlarged every thirty years. Contemporary observers, struck with their magnificence, have naïvely exaggerated the importance of their population. It is absolutely impossible that Ypres in 1247 should have had 200,000 inhabitants, but serious evidence permits the belief that the total of 50,000 may have been reached about this time by Ghent and no doubt by Bruges, and that, by what is known of population in the Middle Ages, is an extraordinarily high figure. It is almost certain that at this period the areas in the basin of the Scheldt already possessed the character which they bear today of being the most densely populated region in Europe.[17]

The feeding of such large urban populations was a very delicate

---

[17] Naturally there are no precise figures except for the end of the Middle Ages. See H. Pirenne, "Les dénombrements de la population d'Ypres au XVe siècle," in *Vierteljahrschrift für Social und Wirtschaftsgeschichte* (1903), 1 *seq.*, and the introduction by J. Cuvelier in his edition of *Dénombrements des foyers en Brabant au XIVe et au XVe siècles* (Brussels, 1912).

problem. The products of the soil in the neighbourhood could not suffice, and indispensable supplies had to be brought from a distance. It was, no doubt, this necessity, as well as the desire to assist commercial transport, which led to the numerous canal undertakings carried out in Flanders in the course of the thirteenth century.[18] Even so, the towns could not be fed without recourse to foreign supplies. As Count Guy de Dampierre stated in 1297,[19] *"la Flandre ne se peut suffire si d'ailleurs ne lui vient,"* and from this time onward she depended for food on the corn from Artois and from the Baltic which was brought to Bruges in the course of commerce. Generalizations must not be drawn from the state of Flanders. Brabant was in a similar condition, but Hainault in the South and Holland in the North cannot be compared with it. Hainault had only two important towns, Tournai and Valenciennes, while in Holland, up to the fifteenth century, Utrecht and Dordrecht were of much less importance than the towns of Flanders and Brabant, and Rotterdam and Amsterdam were still fishing villages. The economic expansion of the Northern Netherlands only began in the Burgundian period, and throughout all the Middle Ages it was surpassed in all branches by that of Belgium.

V

The birth of towns naturally exerted a profound influence on the country. It brought about there an entire transformation which became the more rapid and complete as urban life developed. The economic system of the manor was, as we have seen above, a system devoid of markets. Production was directed towards subsistence only because there were no buyers. It was not principle but necessity which gave it that self-sufficing character which current theory has fixed upon as a natural and primitive characteristic. In reality, far from being a primitive system it was a decadent system. Its only cause was the weakening of commerce, and its disappearance was bound to result from commercial revival. The régime of large estates, which had become more and more common from the end of the Roman period, had had the result of reducing the peasants to a state of serfdom. On both lay and ecclesiastical manors there were only serfs liable to services and to irredeemable dues fixed by custom for their lord's profit. The two essential features of the manorial economy were thus the absence of production for the outside world and a state of serfdom for the inhabitants. Both disappeared under the influence of the towns.

---

[18] *Essays in Mediæval History presented to T. F. Tout,* 139, *seq.*
[19] Kervyn de Lettenhove, *Histoire de Flandre,* II, 560.

The collection within their walls of an increasing population which must live on provisions brought from outside provided the country producers with the markets which they had previously lacked. The peasants did not fail to profit by the certainty of being able to sell their produce. They no longer worked only for themselves, the surplus which they produced at their *mansi* was sold to the inhabitants of the neighbouring town. The rent of land went up considerably, and the methods of cultivation improved, but instead of benefiting from this new situation the proprietors of the soil suffered from it. While their serfs grew rich they grew poor. The rising price of provisions, due not only to increase in demand but also to the fall in the value of money, caused by the fact that commerce was making money plentiful, brought about a crisis in which they were the only people to suffer; for their customary revenues remained fixed, while the cost of living rose incessantly. To deal with this deplorable situation, they resorted to two obvious expedients—one was to give up the old manorial system, to free their serfs, and to modify the system of tenure which had persisted hitherto so as to bring it into relation with the new condition; the second consisted in increasing their resources by enlarging the area of cultivated land. These transformations were facilitated by the growth of the rural population after the disasters caused by the invasions of the Northmen. This growth may be observed from the end of the eleventh century, and evidence for it may be seen in the establishment of a number of men from Flanders and the neighbouring districts in England after the Conquest of 1066, and the extensive participation of the Belgians in the First Crusade.[20] In the twelfth century this movement towards emigration was particularly directed to Germany, where Dutch and Flemish colonists went to cultivate the marshes on the banks of the Lower Elbe.[21] But the increasing population found work to do within the country. The princes and large landowners gave them an outlet in the draining and dyking of the inundated regions on the coast and in the clearing of forests and heaths. In the course of the twelfth century the first *polders* were established along the coast and the Lower Scheldt, while many new towns *(villes-neuves)* were founded in Hainault, in the south of Luxembourg and in the sandy *landes* of the Campine; and it was from that date that the extent of the cultivated area began to exceed its dimensions in Roman times. At the same time freedom began to prevail

---

[20] R. H. George, "The Contribution of Flanders to the Conquest of England," in *Revue Belge de philol. et d'hist.* (1926), 81 *seq.*; G. T. Lapsley, "The Flemings in England in the Reign of Henry II.," in *English Historical Review* (1906), 161 *seq.*

[21] J. W. Thomson, "Dutch and Flemish Colonization in Mediæval Germany," in *American Journ. of Sociology,* Vol. XXIV (1918).

among the rural classes. The old system of servitude was abolished in favour of the immigrants who came to settle in the regions which needed clearing, and little by little the traces of serfdom which persisted on the large estates disappeared. At the beginning of the fourteenth century the sheriffs (*échevins*) of Ypres declared "that they had never heard tell of any of the status of serfs." [22]

VI

This end of the thirteenth century may be considered as the moment when the economic evolution, which had begun with the commercial revival about 300 years earlier, reached its culminating point. All its implications had been realized and it had transformed the organization of society. Now appeared a phenomenon analogous to that which occurred after the industrial revolution of the nineteenth century; new problems arose, and a period in which the question of distribution became acute succeeded one of continuous increase in wealth. The question appeared all the more pressing because progress had been so great, and the particular acerbity with which it was contested in the Netherlands bears witness to the fact that they had obtained an advantage over neighbouring countries similar to that which England had obtained over the rest of Europe in 1830. In this respect, only Italy presented a similar spectacle in mediæval times. But the resemblance is only in fundamentals; the details in the two cases were very different, and to understand those of the earlier period it must be remembered that the industry of the Netherlands was essentially an export industry. Only a very small part of the copper of Dinant, the cloth of Flanders and of Brabant was intended for local consumption. They were manufactured for export, and the result was that their importance continually increased as the export trade developed. From Bruges foreign merchants carried them more and more widely through Europe, and they were among the commodities to be found at all the markets in the interior and at all the ports from Smyrna to Dantzig. It may easily be understood what a contrast such a situation created between the artisans of the great manufacturing centres of the Netherlands and those of almost all the other towns of Western Europe. Instead of working, like the latter, for a clientèle restricted to the bourgeoisie and peasants of the neighbourhood, the workers of the Netherlands produced for international commerce. Elsewhere, the number of industrial workers was forcibly limited by the narrow limits of the markets; in the Netherlands, on the contrary, the market knew no bounds,

---

[22] Beugnot, *Les Olim.*, II, 770.

and the number of artisans grew incessantly. From the end of the thirteenth century the number of men employed in the woollen industry in the principal cities of Flanders, weavers, millers, shearers, dyers, etc., much surpassed the total of those engaged in all the other crafts; and if account is taken of their wives and children they represented more than half the total population. These towns, therefore, present an appearance foreshadowing that of the English industrial towns at the end of the eighteenth century. The greater part of the workers were completely unlike the classic type of mediæval artisan, the small independent master selling his clients goods manufactured from raw material which he owned, and keeping the profit for himself. They must, on the contrary, be regarded as mere wage-earners, working at home for a master, who provided them with raw material and received it back in manufactured form. No doubt these wage-earners differed from those of modern times by their grouping in craft associations (*corporations*). They were not isolated in face of their employers, but that did not prevent the export industries from presenting a clearly capitalist character, and the artisans depended closely on the merchants who provided them with raw material and fixed their wages. The dependence was all the greater because the merchants not only dominated the workers by their economic superiority, but also ruled them by their political authority. In every town the municipal government was exclusively in their hands, and it was, therefore, the class which gave out work which made the rules for the regulation of industry, and that so effectively, that, both in law and in fact, labour was subordinated to capital. Such a situation could only be maintained by force. It lasted so long as the *bonnes gens,* the wealthy men who had usurped the power and used it to their own advantage, succeeded in retaining the monopoly of it. But from the beginning of the thirteenth century this class had to struggle with a continually fiercer opposition. In all the manufacturing towns of the Netherlands there was a struggle between two parties—the common people *(het gemeen)* and the aristocracy, the "small" and the "great," the "bad" and the "good." Everywhere, round the workers in the large industries who were the leaders of the movement, was formed a group of all those whose opposition had been aroused by the increasing exclusiveness of the aristocracy. The artisans in the smaller crafts, and even a section of the richer citizens and merchants whom the dominant class had deprived of all voice in commercial business, supported the efforts of the wage-earners. Political motives thus reinforced the opposition based on social grounds, for it was social and economic grievances above all which kept up the resentment felt by the industrial workers. They complained of the insufficiency of their wages, of the abuse of power by their masters, of frauds in payment and of truck; and strikes broke out among them, of which the earliest are mentioned under the name of *takehans* at Douai in 1245.[23] In 1274 the weavers and fullers of Ghent, in exasperation at the regulations laid down for them by the *échevins,* left the town and retired to Brabant, where the common people and the aristocracy were also at daggers drawn.[24] In the neighbourhood of Liège the same struggle was going on between the "big" and the "little," and at Dinant in 1255 the copper beaters rose against the wealthy class.[25]

The greatness of the danger may be appreciated from the means taken to deal with it. The *échevins* of the aristocracy defended themselves with a vigour as great as that with which they were attacked. They forbade the weavers and fullers to bear arms or even to carry their tools into the streets, to meet in an assembly of more than seven, or to meet at all for any other reason than the business of the craft. They were prodigal of the severest punishments—banishment and death. They concluded agreements between towns, under which they stipulated for the extradition of artisans who had taken refuge in another town after engaging in a conspiracy at home. These measures only increased social bitterness, and vague ideas of communism spread among the poorer people who were threatened by them. In 1280 a general rebellion broke out in almost all the Flemish towns, as the result, perhaps of a concerted movement, perhaps of the swiftness with which the contagion spread to Bruges, Ypres, Douai and Tournai. The intervention of the King of France accentuated the crisis. One night in 1302 the common people of Bruges massacred the French knights whom the aristocracy had called to their aid, and a few months later, on July 2, the army, which Philippe le Bel had sent to avenge this insult, was defeated under the walls of Courtrai by a Flemish army, composed for the most part of woollen workers. This unexpected triumph gave the industrial workers a knowledge of their power, and provoked a general rebellion in Flanders, Brabant and the district of

---

[23] G. Espinas, "Jehan Boine Broke, bourgeois et drapier douaisien," *Vierteljahrschrift für Social und Wirtschaftsgeschichte* (1904). The sources for the history of the Flemish woollen industry have been collected by G. Espinas and H. Pirenne, *Recueil de documents relatifs à l'histoire de l'industrie drapière en Flandre* (Brussels, 1906–24), 4 vols. For Holland must be added N. Posthumus, *Bronnen tot de geschiedenis van de Leidsche Textielnijverheid,* Vol. I (1333–1480), The Hague, 1910. *Cf.* N. Posthumus, *De geschiedenis van de Leidsche Lakenindustrie,* Vol. I, The Hague, 1908, and G. Espinas, *La draperie dans la Flandre française au Moyen-Age,* Paris, 2 vols., 1923; G. Des Marez, *L'organisation du travail à Bruxelles au XVe siècle,* 186 *seq.,* Brussels, 1904. See also *ibid.,* "A charter of Louvain dated 1290," where *"textoribus et aliis operariis pro mercede diurna operatibus"* are mentioned.

[24] Espinas and Pirenne, *Recueil,* II, 21, 92, 94, 379 *seq.*

[25] H. Pirenne, *Histoire de la constitution de la ville de Dinant au moyen-age,* 37 *seq.* (Ghent, 1889).

Liège. It was the starting-point of a period of unrest, which did not terminate until the beginning of the fifteenth century, and which ended the plutocratic régime which up to that time had prevailed in the towns. In spite of reactionary movements on the part of the aristocracy, undertaken in the hope of restoring the past, the arrival of the common people at municipal power was accomplished more or less completely and rapidly in all the districts where an export industry was carried on. It was only rarely, and for a very short time, that the artisans succeeded in obtaining exclusive possession of power. Generally the government was divided between the craftsmen and the aristocracy in constantly changing proportions, and almost everywhere a system was arrived at which gave a place to each social group of which the whole body of citizens were composed, and which approximated fairly well to what might be called a representation of interests.

It must further be noticed that this system nowhere succeeded in assuring a stable and peaceful equilibrium between the parties. No period was more disturbed than that during which the urban democracy triumphed. The cause of this unrest must be sought in the heterogeneous composition of the "common people." Not only were the interests of the small craftsmen (bakers, butchers, blacksmiths, etc.) different from those of the artisans in the export industries, but even the latter were divided into rival groups, and there was perpetual strife between weavers and fullers which periodically resulted in sanguinary conflicts. The wage question had not been settled by the fall of the aristocracy, and the democratic revolution had not deprived industry of its capitalistic organization. Nor had the attainment of political power given the artisans economic independence; they were still wage-earners. The very fact that they produced not for local consumption but for export put them at the mercy of those crises affecting international commerce which they were equally unable to prevent or to understand. They were freed from the domination of the aristocracy, but they were still dependent on the capitalist merchants who provided them with work.[26] They tried at least to reserve the monopoly of such work strictly to themselves. They made every effort to crush outside competition as completely as possible. Ghent, Bruges and Ypres laid their surrounding neighbourhoods under an extraordinary régime of industrial exclusiveness. Military expeditions were organized to search the villages and destroy any tools for the manufacture of cloth. The industry of the small towns was strictly controlled by the large ones, who in the name of pretended "privileges," which were only an abuse of force, prevented them from imitating their own species of woollen goods. The same scene was witnessed on the Meuse, where

---

[26] H. Pirenne, *Belgian Democracy, Its Early History* (1915), 162 *seq.*

Dinant and Bouvigne struggled violently over the industry of copper beating.

VII

This protectionism gone mad did not, however, prevent the industry of the towns from falling into decay. The high scale of wages raised the price of cloth and gradually diminished its sale. At the same time English wool grew scarcer and rose in price, from the day when England, in the course of the fourteenth century, became in its turn a woollen-manufacturing country. To meet this formidable competition it was obviously necessary to reform the industrial régime, obtain wool from Spain and adopt new methods of manufacture, but the artisans saw salvation only in a more and more fervent system of protection. They trusted in nothing but privilege, and, as the situation became more critical, they made it worse by the continually more exclusive regulations by which they tried to ensure for themselves the work which was leaving them. Towards the end of the fourteenth century it was obvious that this short-sighted policy was condemned. Favoured by the capitalists and protected by the Count of Flanders, the rural woollen manufacture, in spite of the protests of the large towns, began to develop to their detriment. Free from "privileges" and from control, it grew in freedom, substituted Spanish for English wool, was content with lower wages and devoted itself to the manufacture of "says," light, cheap stuffs, which gradually took the place which had been held in commerce by the old-fashioned goods made in the towns.[27] From the end of the twelfth century the transformation of commerce was parallel to that of industry. Bruges became more and more an international port, where traffic was concentrated in the hands of the foreign merchants who gathered there from North and South. Besides the Italians, who played the principal part, Britons, Gascons, Basques and Spaniards were to be met there, and there, too, the German Hansa had established its most important base, through which trade relations were kept up between the North Sea and the Baltic on the one hand and the Mediterranean on the other.[28] On the other hand, Flemish

---

[27] H. Pirenne, "Une crise industrielle au XVIe siècle, La draperie urbane et la nouvelle draperie en Flandre," in *Bullet. de l'Acad. Royale de Belgique,* Classe de Lettres, 1905, 489 *seq.*

[28] W. Stein, *Die Genossenschaft der deutschen Kaufleute zu Brügge* (Berlin, 1890); K. Bahr, *Handel und Verkehr der deutschen Hanse in Flandern während des XIV Jahrhunderts* (Leipzig, 1911). For the relations between Bruges and the southern countries see Gilliodts van Severen, *Cartulaire de l'ancien Consulat d'Espagne à Bruges* (1280–1550) (Bruges, 2 vols., 1901–2); and *id., Cartulaire de l'Ancienne estaple de Bruges* (Bruges, 1904–6), 4 vols.

shipping, which had still been numerous in the thirteenth century, had given way in the port to foreign vessels. The galleys of Genoa and Venice, which, from the beginning of the fourteenth century, arrived direct through the Straits of Gibraltar, met there the *coggen* of all the German towns from Dantzig to Hamburg. All the "big business" was now done between the cosmopolitan clientèle which met at Bruges. The natives themselves hardly took part except as commission agents. Their trade, the size of which was now beyond their ability to carry on, clearly assumed a passive character.[29]

At the beginning of the fifteenth century Bruges reached the zenith of its splendour, but afterwards she began to show signs of decadence. The silting up of the Zwyn, at the base of which the city was built, had become gradually worse since the twelfth century. The harbour was continually being moved further downstream, first to Damme, then to Hoek, to Monikereede, finally to Ecluse. But Ecluse itself was affected, and large vessels had to stop at Rammekens on the coast of Zeeland and land their cargoes in small boats. Besides these deplorable material conditions, there prevailed an outworn economic organization, which fidelity to tradition prevented the citizens from changing. They were just as incapable of adapting themselves to new conditions in commerce as were the manufacturing towns to those in industry. Instead of trying to make up for the disadvantages of their situation by a more liberal and pliable régime which would induce foreigners to remain, they thought only of exploiting the trade by which they lived in proportion as it declined. They remained faithful to the economic system which had made them great in the Middle Ages, and failed to understand that times had changed, and that, in proportion as the volume and intensity of commerce increased, its continued limitation under a worn-out system of regulation became impossible. They tried to force foreign merchants to frequent Bruges, and obtained from the Dukes of Burgundy a decree imposing the obligation of continued residence in the city. But though the Dukes gave them the decrees they asked for, it was with continually less personal interest in the matter; their personal activity was devoted in the utmost degree to encouraging the growing prosperity of Antwerp, where, in striking contrast to Bruges, the economic liberty which was ensuring the success of the country woollen manufacture in Flanders exercised a continuous attraction for foreigners. The excellent situation of the port, deeply land-locked and far removed from the dangers of North Sea pirates, added another advantage to those which already combined to seduce

---

[29] Neither Bruges nor any other town in Flanders or the rest of Belgium was a member of the German Hansa, with the sole exception of the Walloon town of Dinant, which was affiliated to it in order to participate in the privileges which the German merchants enjoyed in England. See H. Pirenne, *Dinant,* 97 *seq.*

them from Bruges. The contrast between Antwerp and Bruges is one between the past and the future, between privilege and equal rights, between protection and free trade.

The Dukes of Burgundy, who had just united under their sceptre the various principalities of the Netherlands (1419–77), facilitated the transition from mediæval to modern economic organization. They undertook the struggle against both political and economic privileges, and rightly proclaimed themselves the defenders of "common good" against "private good." It was no longer local but general interests which inspired them. In Holland they energetically upheld against the German Hansa that movement towards maritime development which was destined to succeed so brilliantly. They created a common monetary system for all the provinces, and protected both the country woollen manufacture against the protests of Ghent and Ypres, and the commerce of Antwerp against the opposition of Bruges. Their accession marks the end of the mediæval period of Netherlands history and the beginning of that modern period which saw the rise to fame first of Antwerp and then of Amsterdam.

Some Suggested Readings

Bolin, Sture. "Mohammed, Charlemagne and Ruric," *Scandinavian Economic History Review,* I (1953), 5–39.

Dennett, Jr., Daniel C. "Pirenne and Mohammed," *Speculum,* XXIII (1948), 165–90.

Ganshof, François Louis. "Henri Pirenne and Economic History," *The Economic History Review,* VI (1936), 179–85.

Hirshler, Eric. "Medieval Economic Competition," *Journal of Economic History,* XIV (1954), 52–58.

Postan, Michael M. "The Rise of a Money Economy," *The Economic History Review,* XIV (1944), 123–34.

An Industrial Revolution of the Thirteenth Century*

E. M. Carus-Wilson

It has been commonly supposed that the thirteenth century witnessed a decline in the nascent cloth industry of England, a decline which was only to be checked and converted into renewed advance and yet more spectacular progress under the vigorous patronage of Edward III.[1] We read, for instance, of the "impoverished state" of the industry "on the eve of the great experiment"; of how "something was wrong with the industry, and if it was to be given fresh life something must be done."[2] Such a conception of arrested growth and even decay is not, however, borne out by a close investigation of the sources. On the contrary, they reveal rather the expansion and rapid development of the industry up to the eve of the accession of Edward III. The reason for this discrepancy is not that the sources themselves have been misinterpreted, but that only one group of them, the urban records, has been hitherto explored in this connection. It has been too readily assumed that the history of industry in England at this time was to be found in the history of her towns and their gilds, and that symptoms of decline evident here signified a decline in the industry as a whole. In reality, however, rural records also throw a flood of light on the industrial history of the time, and when they are considered in conjunction with those of the towns it becomes apparent

---

* Reprinted from *The Economic History Review*, Vol. XI (1941), by permission of the publisher and the author.

[1] Owing to war conditions it proved impossible to check and to complete all the references in this article, particularly those to manuscript sources in the custody of the Public Record Office.

[2] E. Lipson, *The History of the English Woollen and Worsted Industries* (1921), 11; *cf.* E. Lipson, *The Economic History of England*, 7th edn. (1937), 449–50; L. F. Salzman, *English Industries of the Middle Ages* (1923), 203.

41

that the century was one of striking progress industrially, though of equally striking change and upheaval. It witnessed, in fact, an industrial revolution due to scientific discoveries and changes in technique; a revolution which brought poverty, unemployment and discontent to certain old centres of the industry, but wealth, opportunity and prosperity to the country as a whole, and which was destined to alter the face of medieval England.

In the early Middle Ages the various processes of cloth-making were all strictly "handcrafts." The chief processes, apart from dyeing and finishing, were four. First the wool was carded or combed by hand; then it was spun on the rock or distaff. Next the yarn thus prepared was woven on a loom worked by hand and foot, and finally the loose "web" thus made was fulled by hand or foot. The process of fulling, that is to say, of beating or compressing the cloth in water, served first of all to shrink the cloth, reducing it in width by anything from a fifth to a half, and in length to a corresponding extent.[3] This so increased the density and weight per unit of length as to give it much greater resistance to weather and wear. Secondly, it served to "felt" the cloth, so inextricably entangling the fibres that the pattern of the weaving often ceased to be visible. This not only gave the cloth greater fabric strength, but also a smoother and softer surface, and it was an essential preliminary to the finishing processes of raising and shearing applied to the finer cloths. In addition to shrinking and felting the cloth, making it close and firm, the fulling process also scoured it and cleansed it, with the aid of various detergents[4] such as fuller's earth, removing especially the oil with which the wool had been impregnated before spinning. Now the mechanising of the first three cloth-making processes during the eighteenth and nineteenth centuries is a commonplace of history, but the mechanising of the fourth during the thirteenth century, though it gave rise to an industrial revolution not less remarkable, has attracted scarcely any attention. It is with this that the present article proposes to deal.

Three primitive methods of fulling "by might and strength of man," without any mechanism, have been most commonly used in western Europe: beating with the feet, with the hands, or with clubs wielded by hand. Most suited to long heavy broadcloths is some method of fulling by foot such as is vividly portrayed in the paintings

---

[3] For the purpose and nature of fulling, see J. and J. C. Schofield, *The Finishing of Wool Goods* (1935), and J. Schofield, *The Science and Practice of Scouring and Milling* (1921). The medieval assize of cloth sometimes quoted a different standard for cloth "watered" and cloth "unwatered," *e.g.* 11 Hen. VI, c.9.

[4] *Cf.* G. Espinas, "Essai sur la Technique de l'Industrie Textile à Douai aux xiiie et xive siècles," *Mémoires de la Société nationale des Antiquaires de France*, t. LXVIII (1909), 42.

on the piers of the *fullonica* at Pompeii, and in those of the house of the Vettii there. In these we can see the fuller at work, standing almost naked in a trough, trampling the cloth under foot, while his hands rest on low side walls by which he can support and raise himself. Traces of what may have been fulleries such as these in Roman Britain have been revealed in three places: at Titsey and Darenth in Kent, and at Chedworth in Gloucestershire. Here we have found very similar troughs, circular in form, with low side walls and drainage facilities.[5] Their close proximity, in each case, to beds of fuller's earth and to what later became flourishing centres of the industry, would seem to lend some support to the theory that they were fulleries, though the matter cannot be considered as finally determined. From Roman Gaul we have an actual representation of a fuller at work in a trough, carved on the "fuller's tomb" at Sens.[6] So for a thousand years and more fullers trod the cloth underfoot, as indeed they have continued to do in outlying parts, such as the Hebrides, untouched by the mechanical inventions of the thirteenth or of the eighteenth centuries. The early fourteenth century ordinances of the fullers' gilds both at Lincoln and at Bristol mention this working "in the trough."[7] and later on in *Piers Plowman* we read of cloth that is "fulled under fote."[8]

Sometimes hands were used instead of, or in addition to, feet. A visitor to Skye in 1774 thus described the Luaghad, or fulling of cloth, there: "Twelve or fourteen women, divided into equal numbers, sit down on each side of a long board ribbed lengthways, placing the cloth on it: first they begin to work it backwards and forwards with their hands, singing at the same time as at the quern: when they have tired their hands, every female uses her feet for the same purpose, and six or seven pairs of naked feet are in the most violent agitation, working one against the other: as by this time they grow very earnest in their labours, the fury of the song rises; at length it arrives to such a pitch that without breach of charity you would imagine a troop of female demoniacs to have been assembled."[9]

Hand fulling alone, or fulling with clubs wielded by hand, has probably always been used for smaller articles. Indeed methods of

---

[5] *Archaelogia,* LIX (1904), G. E. Fox, "Notes on some probable traces of Roman Fulling in Britain," 208–9; *Guide to Chedworth Roman Villa* (1926), 12–13.

[6] C. Roach-Smith, *Collectanea Antiqua,* V (1861), Plate XX, Fig. 1.

[7] Toulmin Smith, *English Gilds* (1870), 180, *in alveo; Little Red Book of Bristol,* ed. F. B. Bickley (1900), II, 12, *ouveraunt en le stok.*

[8] *Piers Plowman* (B), XV, 445. Angus Pirie, a skilled weaver of Dornoch, used to full his cloth by foot in a trough but has given up this method as too strenuous and too chilling now that he is old.

[9] Quoted in E. Lipson, *History of the English Woollen and Worsted Industries* (1921), 139.

fulling even in the same locality seem commonly to have varied according to the size and character of the articles to be fulled. A traveller to Iceland in 1814–15 thus describes two different methods in vogue there: "Both ends being knocked out of a barrel, it is filled with articles to be fulled, when it is laid on the side, and two men lie down on their backs, one at either end, with their feet in the barrel, and literally *walk* the cloth, by kicking it against each other. Smaller articles they full by placing them between their knees and breast, and then moving backwards and forwards with the body, turning them always with their hands till ready. This accounts for the very awkward motion which the Icelanders almost always fall into when sitting, and from which many of them cannot refrain even in church."[10] In France in the eighteenth century fulling by hand was frequently used for hosiery, and fulling with clubs wielded by hand for hats and caps.[11] We may infer a similar use of clubs in Roman times from the account of the martyrdom of St. James the Less, written in the second century: *Quidam autem ex eis, accepto fuste ex officina fullonis, quo comprimebat vestes, valide infligit ejus capiti.*[12] For this reason the fuller's club became the emblem of St. James and is to be seen in many medieval representations of him, as for instance in the east window of Gloucester Cathedral, on the rood screen at Ranworth, on one of the stall panels at Blythburgh, and on the font at Stalham.[13]

In medieval records it is not easy to distinguish this method of using clubs from that of fulling by hand alone, since both could be described as "fulling by hand" in distinction to "fulling by foot." At any rate it seems that in England one or other of these methods of hand fulling was commonly used for hats and caps. Thus in London long after mechanical fulling had commonly been adopted for broadcloths, the Hurers successfully petitioned against this method being allowed for hats and caps, and ordinances were passed to this effect in 1376;[14] several citizens were fined for breach of the ordinance and, during the hearing of a case against one John Godefray, a jury of cappers and hatters declared that caps could not and ought not to be fulled under the feet or in any other way than by the hands of men.[15]

---

[10] E. Henderson, *Iceland* (Edinburgh, 1818), I, 365.

[11] Savary des Bruslons, *Dictionnaire Universel de Commerce,* II, 526; Postlethwayt, *Universal Dictionary of Trade and Commerce* (4th edn., 1774): "Fulling."

[12] *Acta Sanctorum,* XIV, 35.

[13] For other examples, see C. Cahier, *Caractéristiques des saints dans l'art populaire* (1867), 547; F. C. Husenbeth, *Emblems of Saints,* 3rd edn., ed. A. Jessopp (1882), 110.

[14] *Memorials of London,* ed. H. T. Riley, (1868), 400.

[15] *Calendar of Plea and Memoranda Rolls, 1364–1381,* ed. A. H. Thomas (1929), 230, 233; *Memorials of London, ut supra,* 529.

It is clear that the hatters and cappers were as much opposed to fulling by foot as to mechanical fulling; thus again in 1404 they petitioned that their work should not be fulled in mills *or by feet*, but only by the hands of men, and again offending citizens were punished.[16] Most probably hand fulling was reserved for small articles such as hats and caps, made usually of felt, while the long, heavy broadcloths which came to form the staple of the English export industry were fulled by foot.

Such were the primitive methods of fulling in use when the English woollen industry was first established. Most important of them is fulling by foot, since this method was applied to the long, heavy broadcloth which came to form the staple of the English export industry.

The mechanical method of fulling invented during the Middle Ages, and in use for many centuries, was evolved from the primitive method of fulling by foot. The invention was a twofold one. In the first place the action of the two feet was replaced by that of two wooden hammers, alternately raised and dropped on the cloth as it lay in the trough, and controlled probably by a revolving drum on the tilt- or lift-hammer system.[17] In the second place this revolving drum was attached to the spindle of a water-wheel, and this supplied the motive power. Thus, by a simple contrivance, water power was made to replace human labour, and a series of hammers could be set to work with but one man standing by to watch the cloth and see that it was kept properly moving in the trough. The whole was then spoken of as a *molendinum fullericum,* or "fulling mill."[18] since, though it was not strictly a mill *(molendinum)* in that it did not grind *(molere)*, it bore a resemblance in one part of its mechanism to the water corn mill. Indeed the building itself, down by the water, with its leet and its revolving wheel, would be difficult to distinguish externally from a corn mill. Henceforth, just as there had hitherto been a distinction in rentals, surveys, etc., between the windmill, the watermill and the horse-mill *(molendinum ventricum, molendinum aquaticum,* and *molendinum ad equos),* so now there appears a further distinction between the water *corn* mill and the water *fulling* mill *(molendinum aquaticum blaericum* and *molendinum aquaticum fullericum).*

---

16 *Ibid.,* 667.

17 This revolving drum could be turned by hand, and such a device may still be seen in use in parts of Scotland today, though it is very heavy to work.

18 While "fulling mill" is the most widely used term, certain parts of England had their own local terms, derived from words of different origins describing the same fulling process. Thus in the place of "full," "fuller," "fulling mill," we find "tuck," "tucker," "tucking mill" in the west country, especially in Cornwall, Devon and Somerset; and "walk," "walker," "walking mill" (or "walkmill") in the north, especially in the Lake District, while in Wales a fulling mill becomes a "pandy." Many of the sites of these ancient mills can be identified by the fact that they have one or other of these expressions attached to them.

The question now arises as to the date of the invention of the water fulling mill. This would seem impossible to fix with any certainty. M. Bloch asserts that there was a fulling mill at Grenoble "about 1050,"[19] but the actual evidence does not seem to support his conclusion. The charter to which he refers speaks of certain rights *in unum quodque molendinum, quando edificatur, et in bateorium, similiter quando edificatur.*[20] Now a *bateorium, battorium, batatorium* or *baptitorium* is certainly a place where beating or hammering is carried on, but we are not justified in assuming that this beating was done by water power, or that it was necessarily the beating of cloth. Ducange defines *Bateria* as, *Ars tundendi pannos, terendi cortices et alia similia facienda,* and in a charter quoted by him there are enumerated *furnos, torcularia, molendina, baptitoria, et fullonos.* Clearly, then a *baptitorium* or *bateorium* is not even synonymous with a fullery, much less with a mechanical fulling *mill,* and there is as yet no evidence that the fulling mill was known on the continent at that date.[21] In England, at any rate, it seems as though water fulling mills were introduced in the latter part of the twelfth century. The earliest reference to one so far discovered is that in the survey of the Templars' lands made in 1185. This mentions a *molendinum fulerez* at Newsham in Yorkshire and another, built by the Templars themselves, at Barton, close to Temple Guiting, in the Cotswolds.[22] Four years later a charter to the Abbey of Stanley in Wilts speaks of the *molendinum monachorum fullericum.*[23] The absence so far of any earlier references to fulling mills does not, of course, prove their non-existence, and how far the lack of other evidence for the twelfth and other centuries is due to lack of documents comparable to those of later centuries it is impossible to say. But a significant change in nomenclature points also to the change having been introduced in the late twelfth century. For from the opening of the thirteenth century not only do references to such mills increase, but so also does the use of the phrase *corn* mill in distinction to *fulling mill,* while the word *fullonia* disappears, giving place to

---

[19] *Annales d'histoire économique et sociale,* no. 36, November 1935, M. Bloch, "Avènement et conquêtes du moulin à eau," 543.

[20] *Cartulaires de l'Église Cathédrale de Grenoble,* ed. M. J. Marion (Paris, 1869), 119.

[21] See Postscript.

[22] R. Dodsworth and Sir W. Dugdale, *Monasticon Anglicanum* (1655–73), II, 540; B. A. Lees, *Records of the Templars in England in the Twelfth Century* (1935), pp. ccxiii, 50, 127, cxxv. There was also a derelict fulling mill at Witham, Essex, in 1308, and this may, it is suggested, represent the "mill" in the survey of 1185, *ibid.,* p. lxxix.

[23] W. de G. Birch, *Collections towards the history of the Cistercian Abbey of Stanley, Wilts* (1876), 43, quoting Brit. Mus. Harleian MS. 84, f. 273b; see also 15, 17, 33, for later references.

molendinum fullericum. Certainly the fulling mill cannot have been at all widely used until the thirteenth century, and it is in the late thirteenth century that we come across the first evidence of opposition to its use on the part of the handworkers.

The origin of the invention is even more obscure than its date. We know neither in what country, nor by whom, water power was first applied to fulling, nor whether the idea spread from a common source or was evolved independently in different regions. It is conceivable that the Templars may have introduced the fulling mill into England. At any rate the religious orders were among the first to take advantage of it and to develop its possibilities. In monastic cartularies many early references, not all of which can be precisely dated, are to be found to fulling mills. About the year 1200 the Abbey of Winchcomb possessed a fulling mill at "Clively," and when the Abbot made a grant of another mill it was on condition that it should not be converted into a fulling mill to compete with his own.[24] The monks of Evesham held a fullers' mill *(molendinum fullonum)* at Bourton-on-the-Water in Gloucestershire in 1206;[25] the Augustinian friary of St. John the Baptist at Ludlow had one before 1221, probably on the Teme;[26] Newminster had one on the Wansbeck very early in its history;[27] St. Albans had established one by 1274,[28] and in an extent of the Abbey of Kirkstall of 16 Edward I a fulling mill is mentioned as well as a tanning mill.[29]

Nor were the great episcopal estates behind the monastic ones. The earliest Pipe Roll of the Bishop of Winchester (1208–9) shows that he then possessed four fulling mills (described as *fulleraticum* and *foleraticum)*: at Waltham, Sutton, Brightwell and New Alresford; mills to which Dr. Hubert Hall called attention as "perhaps the earliest fulling mills in England of which we have mention." [30] Later rolls show the Bishop possessed of a fulling mill at Downton in Wiltshire by 1215, of two in Oxfordshire, at Witney, by 1223, and of one in Somerset, at Taunton, by 1224.[31] The Bishop of Bath owned a fulling

---

[24] *Monasterium Beatae Mariae Virginis et Sancti Cenhelmi: Landboc,* ed. D. Royce (1892), I, 195.

[25] *Chronicon Abbatiae Eveshamensis,* ed. W. D. Macray (Rolls Series, 1863), 213.

[26] Harleian MS. 6690, f. 89 *et seq.,* quoted in T. Wright, *History of Ludlow* (1852), 98.

[27] *Newminster Cartulary* (Surtees Soc., LXVI, 1878), 3.

[28] *Washingham, Gesta Abbatum Monasterii Sancti Albani,* ed. H. T. Riley (Rolls Series, 1867), I, 410 *et seq.*

[29] P.R.O. Ancient Extents 86 (1).

[30] *Pipe Roll of the Bishop of Winchester,* ed. Hubert Hall (1903), pp. xxvii, 1, 13, 41, 61.

[31] P.R.O. Ecclesiastical Commission, Various, II, 159273, 159278 *et seq.* References given by Miss M. Wretts-Smith.

mill at Kidderminster in 1293,[32] while early in the following century the Bishop of Exeter agreed to join with the Mayor and Commonalty of Barnstaple in erecting mills, including fulling mills, on the river which divided their property.[33]

It must not, however, be assumed that, since many of the earliest surviving references are to mills on monastic and ecclesiastical estates, laymen lagged behind. Indeed in the monastic cartularies themselves we get glimpses of lay owners of fulling mills, for such mills often happened to be part of endowments bestowed by laymen upon a monastery. About the year 1200, for instance, Robert of Seckworth owned two "myllis fuleree" in Seckworth and granted the tithes of them to the nunnery of Godstow.[34] Godstow also claimed tithes in 1235 of the mill called "pannmylle" (probably a "cloth mill") at Wycombe.[35] Again, when Peter Undergod founded the hospital of St. John the Baptist near the bridge over the Teme at Ludlow, he endowed it, *inter alia,* with the fulling mill which he had bought from Gilbert de Lacy.[36]

The fulling mills on lay estates for which most early records survive are, not unnaturally, those of the King himself. One of the first royal mills was that near Marlborough, at Elcot. This was in existence in the reign of John and was rebuilt by the King's orders in 1237. The task was entrusted to William de Pretsch and Vincent Carpentar, who had workmen under them, and cost altogether £4 17s. 4d. Most of this money was spent on felling and carting timber from Savernake forest; the rest on remaking the mill-pond, the weir, the mill-wheel and its enclosure, the mill-race and also the *flagella et baterella*— probably the hammers for beating the cloth.[37] In 1251 Henry III ordered a fulling mill to be built in his park at Guildford;[38] the royal manor of Steeple Langford in Wilts had one in 1294,[39] and by the beginning of the following century there was a royal fulling mill in the West Riding at Knaresborough.[40]

When we turn to trace fulling mills on estates other than monastic,

[32] *Inquisitions Post Mortem for the County of Worcestershire*, edited for the Worcester Historical Society by J. W. Willis Bund (1894), I, 43; *Calendar of Inquisitions Post Mortem*, III, 45 (21 Ed. I).

[33] *Reprint of the Barnstaple Records,* ed. J. A. Chanter and T. Wainwright (1900), I, 110, no. 20.

[34] *The Godstow and Oseney Registers*, ed. A. Clark (Early English Text Society, 1905), I, 43.

[35] *Ibid.,* 89.

[36] Wright, *op. cit.,* 98.

[37] *Calendar of Liberate Rolls*, I, 278; *Great Roll of the Pipe, 1241–1242.* 175; *Rotuli Litterarum Clausarum,* ed. T. D. Hardy (Record Commission, 1833–44), II, 23.

[38] *Calendar of Liberate Rolls*, III, 376; T. H. Turner, *Domestic Architecture in England* (1851), I, 233; (1853), II, 149

[39] P.R.O. Rentals and Surveys, General Series, portf. 16, no. 66.

[40] *Calendar of Close Rolls, 1302–1307,* 35.

episcopal or royal, there is, unfortunately, no comparable evidence available. The sources are on the whole later in date and different in character. The mandates and instructions on Royal Close Rolls and Liberate Rolls have, for instance, no parallel, and in place of the twelfth and early thirteenth century monastic cartularies we have only scattered deeds, scarcely ever so early in date. Nor are there any early consecutive series of manorial accounts such as those enrolled on the great pipe rolls of the Bishop of Winchester or on the royal pipe rolls, but only separate accounts, surviving in fragments. The principal sources are threefold: first the Inquisitions Post Mortem taken on the death of a supposed tenant-in-chief for the information of the King; secondly, Rentals and Custumals of individual manors drawn up for the information of the lord of the manor and his officials; and, thirdly, year to year Accounts kept of the administration of such manors and records of their Courts. These three sources are extensive from the latter part of the thirteenth century, though not until then. The first is the most accessible in print, through the *Calendars of Inquisitions Post Mortem,* but these are deceptive for the present investigation, since they do not always reproduce the detailed extents in which the fulling mills are usually to be found. In these printed calendars, for instance, no fulling mills appear for Wiltshire before the reign of Edward III, but the more detailed *Abstracts of Wiltshire Inquisitions Post Mortem* (1242–1326) give five.[41] Hence, for countries where we have no such thorough survey, the originals must constantly be consulted. It must further be remembered that these inquisitions may not always record the state of affairs at the moment that the return was actually made; they may reproduce earlier surveys. Thus when a fulling mill appears we can only be certain that it existed either at that or at an earlier date. Nor do Rentals and Custumals always give precise dates; often their date can only be inferred from their handwriting, and even then it is possible that they are sometimes copies of earlier surveys. None of these sources is sufficiently comprehensive to form any basis for statistical analysis, but from them and other records we can at least gain an impression of the rapid extension of the fulling mill during the thirteenth century and its widespread distribution at the beginning of the fourteenth century. And it must be borne in mind that the mills of which record has survived can be only a small proportion of the total, and that the present investigation cannot claim in any way to be exhaustive.[42]

. . . .

[41] *Abstracts of Wiltshire Inquisitions Post Mortem,* ed. E. A. Fry (1242–1326) (1908), I, 119, 227, 246, 257, 350.

[42] Further evidence is constantly coming to light, and collections of local deeds still have much to yield. The writer would welcome information as to other early mills than those listed.

From this survey,† inadequate though it must be, it is evident that the use of the fulling mill had become widespread over England and the borders of Wales between the end of the twelfth and the beginning of the fourteenth century. The fulling mill was, indeed, destined to supersede almost entirely the primitive fulling "under the feet of men," though its final triumph was not yet assured, and a veritable revolution in one of the chief branches of cloth manufacture was in progress. Foot fulling was giving way to mechanical fulling; human labour was being displaced by water power; the industry was being carried on at the mill rather than in the home; it was dependent as never before upon considerable capital equipment, and was already passing out of the gild system of control. Moreover, changes in technique and organisation, striking enough in themselves to warrant the use of the word revolution, were giving rise to changes in location no less striking—changes which were to affect the distribution of the whole English woollen industry. For the survey, it will be seen, reveals remarkable concentration of mills in the West Riding of Yorkshire, in the Lake District, in Cornwall, Devon, Somerset and the Cotswolds, in Wilts, and in the Kennet Valley, with a corresponding dearth of mills in the eastern parts of England. Further, it shows that the mills were almost entirely in the country districts rather than in the towns. Now in both these respects a startling change has taken place since the twelfth and thirteenth centuries. Then the chief centres of cloth manufacture were not in the hilly northern and western regions of England but in the eastern lowlands; not in the rural districts but in the cities. York, Beverley, Lincoln, Louth, Stamford and Northampton[43] were then famous for their fine quality cloth, and next to them in importance came London, Oxford, Winchester, Leicester and Colchester. In all these cities there was a large-scale industry supplying London and, in many instances which we can trace, the export market, and many have left record of their organised groups of fullers[44] as well as weavers. Now, however, with the invention of the fulling mill, water power was becoming a decisive factor in the location of the

---

† The text of the original article had a long table twisting well over 100 different fulling mills known to have existed *before the reign of Edward III,* their location, and the archival source which made reference to them. Professor Carus-Wilson has kindly permitted the editors to omit this table.

[43] See *e.g.* Newcastle Records Series, II, *Pleas from Curia Regis and Assize Rolls,* 307; *Calendar of Patent Rolls, 1247–1258,* 309; F. D. Swift, *The Life and Times of James the First . . . of Aragon* (1894), 229; *Calendar of Close Rolls, 1234–1237,* 73, 301; *1247–1251,* 154, 157, 301, 375.

[44] *E.g.* Lincoln, 1200 (*Curia Regis Rolls,* I, 259). Stamford, 1182 (F. Peck, *The Antiquities of Stamford,* 1785, 17). Northampton, 1275 (*Hundred Rolls,* II, 3). London, 1298 (*Liber Custumarum,* ed. H. T. Riley, Rolls Series (1860), I, 128). Leicester, 1260 (*Records of the Borough of Leicester,* ed. M. Bateson (1899), I, 89). Winchester, 1130 (*Pipe Roll, 31 Henry III,* 37).

industry, and it began to concentrate on the swift, clear streams of the north and west, in remote valleys far beyond the bounds of the ancient chartered cities of the plains.

Hence it comes about that this chapter in the development of England's woollen industry is written largely in the records of the manor rather than of the borough. Indeed, in many instances which we can trace, the initiative in the new developments was taken by the lord of the manor, and the capital equipment provided by him. Thus, as we have seen, King Henry III reconstructed his fulling mill at Elcot, using timber from his forest of Savernake,[45] at a cost of £4 17s. 4d., while the Bishop of Winchester built a new fulling mill at Brightwell costing £9 4s. 4d.[46] Similarly the fulling mill at Burnley was built anew (de novo constructo) for £2 12s. 6d. at the expense of the lord of the manor, and money was also spent on the repair of that at Colne.[47] Such instances could be multiplied.

The incentive to such enterprise on the part of the lord of the manor was that the fulling mill was an investment from which considerable profit could be derived. For, like the corn mill, the oven, the wine press, the dye pan, or any other such equipment erected by the lord, it could be made a manorial monopoly, to which the tenants owed suit.[48] Its value varied not only according to its own efficiency, but also according to the size, population and industry of the area it served. Thus, for example, a half share in the fulling mill at Kendal was at one time worth 10 marks a year, but in 1274 its value was considered to have fallen to 8 marks.[49] The reason alleged was that the tenants at Kentmere no longer did suit to it, and probably what had happened was that the mill at Staveley had now been built;[50] and since Staveley is half-way between Kentmere and Kendal, this would mean for the tenants a journey of only about four instead of eight miles down the Kent valley with their cloths. It is perhaps not a mere coincidence that the development of the fulling mill took place during the century which saw the crystallisation and culmination

---

[45] Supra, 48.

[46] Pipe Roll of the Bishop of Winchester, ut supra, 13: in unum molendino foleratico facto de novo (1208–9).

[47] Two Compoti of the Lancashire and Cheshire Manors of Henry de Lacy, 24 and 33 Edward I, Chetham Soc., New Series, CXII (1907), 15, 16.

[48] On this subject see Beiträge zur Geschichte der Technik (1913), C. Koehne, "Die Mühle im Rechte der Völker"; Annales d'histoire économique et sociale, no. 36, ut supra, and cf. G. Espinas, La draperie dans la Flandre française au moyen age (Paris, 1923), II, 213, n. 6: the Duke of Burgundy writes to his receiver concerning his corn mills at Bruay, suggesting that for his greater profit one of them should be made into a "molin foleur de draps."

[49] P.R.O. Inquisitions Post Mortem, Edward I, 5.

[50] [The reference here is to the table of mills which the editors have omitted from the present text.—Publisher.]

of the manorial system with seignorial rights and privileges at their height.

How eagerly such monopolies were coveted may be seen from Jocelin de Brakelond's story of Herbert the Dean, who thought that "the profit which may come from the wind ought to be denied to no man." When Herbert excused himself thus for erecting his own wind-mill the Abbot was speechless with rage, and when Herbert pleaded that it was only to grind his own corn and not for other men's, he retorted, "I thank you as much as if you had cut off both my feet; by the face of God, I will never eat bread until that building be overturned."[51] If even the wind could be thus monopolised, it was still more easy to enforce control over the water, to insist that the lord alone had the right to use it for profit-making, and that no one else could do so without a licence purchased from him. Even before the introduction of the fulling mill, the lord claimed the right to dispose of the watercourse as he pleased for fulling and dyeing, reserv-ing it wholly to himself, or leasing it out, often as a monopoly, to others. Thus for instance at Hadleigh one John Garleberd was granted for an annual rent 10 feet of land along the bank of the mill-pond, with permission to wash his dyed wool there and draw out water, on condition that no one else should have access there.[52] Later on two dyers were fined at Hadleigh for washing dyed wool in the lord's pond without licence.[53] Similarly the cellarer of Bury St. Edmunds claimed the right to prohibit the town fullers from using the water. So profitable were such monopolies that frequently when some measure of freedom was granted to tenants the lord expressly reserved the right to maintain them in his hands. So, for instance, in the charter of 1228 granted by the Archbishop of York to Sherburn in Elmet, the "burgesses in our borough of Shireburn" were forbidden on pain of forfeiture to have an "oven, dye-pan or fulling stocks." Those who made use of the Archbishop's dye-pan might have, in any week they pleased, "a cartload of dead wood from our wood at Shireburn."[54] Or, again, a charter of King John to Ulverston reserved in the King's hands the oven, dye-pan and fullery *(furnum, tinctoriam et fulloniam)*.[55]

[51] *Chronica Jocelini de Brakelonda*, ed. J. G. Rokewode (Camden Soc., Old Series, XIII, 1840), 43; *cf.* the dispute at Hesdin-le-Vieux over the fulling mills of the Prior of S. Georges (G. Espinas and H. Pirenne, *Recueil de documents relatifs à l'histoire de l'industrie drapière en Flandre* [Brussels, 1906–23], II, 690).

[52] P.R.O. Ecclesiastical Commission, Various, I, 16/2.

[53] *Ibid.*, 16/9.

[54] *Old Yorkshire*, 2nd Series, 1885, W. Wheater, "The Ancient Cloth Trade."

[55] T. West, *Antiquities of Furness* (1813), 85, 418; *fulloniam* cannot strictly be interpreted as fulling *mill* as it is here, and often elsewhere, translated: it would seem to denote almost always the primitive non-mechanised fullery, and by the fourteenth century the world has virtually disappeared. *Cf.* charter, quoted by Ducange, reserving *furnos, torcularia, molendina, et fullonos*.

Nor did the lords of the manor claim merely the exclusive right of erecting and possessing such fulleries or fulling mills. They insisted also that all cloth made on the manor must be brought to the manorial mill and there fulled by the new mechanical method, and no longer at home "by hand or foot"; just as they insisted that all corn must be ground in their wind mills or water mills, and not at home by hand mills. Such a claim would seem as difficult to justify as it certainly was to enforce. Never, perhaps, was it wholly conceded, and both manorial court rolls and monastic chronicles bear witness to the constant opposition it aroused, and to the hatred which it inspired. At Hawkesbury, for instance, in 1325–26, one Matilda, daughter of Adam the Carter, was fined for fulling a piece of cloth *alibi quam ad molendinum domini*.[56] Other such cases occur on manorial court rolls, but most striking is the evidence from monastic sources, and most vivid of all is the account of the struggle over the fulling mills at St. Albans in 1274. At this time the abbey of St. Albans was evidently as proud of its mills as of its conventual buildings. Abbot John (1235–60) spent, it is said, no less than £100 on their reconstruction, taking them back into his own hands after they had been leased out at farm and allowed to fall into disrepair. His successors were evidently determined to make a goodly profit out of them and claimed that no grinding of corn or fulling of cloth, even of small pieces,[57] could be carried out anywhere except at the abbey mills. The people of St. Albans, however, resisted what they considered to be an unwarranted usurpation; they gave the abbey mills a wide berth and preferred to grind and full at home, free of charge, by the primitive old-fashioned methods.[58] In 1274 matters came to a head in what the chronicler describes as a great insurrection, provoked by the zeal of Abbot Roger in enforcing his monopolies by entering the houses of offenders and levying distraint. The people of St. Albans determined to contest the case in the King's court, opened a fighting fund to which rich and poor contributed, and, when Queen Eleanor was passing through St. Albans, staged a great demonstration to enlist her support. The Abbot tried to outwit them by diverting the royal route and taking the Queen by a back way to the abbey, but his strategem failed, and the Queen was intercepted by an angry crowd consisting mainly of women,

---

[56] P.R.O. Court Rolls, General Series, 175/41.

[57] *Pannos viles* in contrast to *pannos grossos, i.e.* probably small pieces woven for use at home rather than whole broadcloths woven for sale; this restriction would be peculiarly irksome.

[58] One of the fullers, Henry de Porta, living in Fullers Street, was accused of erecting in his house a *truncum ad fullandum pannos;* this may perhaps imply some partly mechanised device such as wooden hammers attached to a revolving drum worked by hand. Such a device is still used today, *e.g.* in the "Clansman Mills" at Killin. *Cf. supra,* 45.

whose attack, said the monkish chronicler, was formidable "since it is difficult happily to compose the anger of women." Weeping and lamenting and stretching forth their hands, the women complained bitterly of the Abbot's tyranny, crying "Domina, miserere nobis." It was not easy, however, for an English mob to make their grievances intelligible to a foreign queen and her entourage, and the sympathy aroused by their tears seems quickly to have been dispelled by the assurances of the astute Abbot that the light words of such women were really unworthy of credence. At any rate when the people of St. Albans brought their case into the King's court, judgment was given against them, and, despite an appeal, the Abbot won the day and the judgment was proudly entered in the chronicle for future reference.[59]

The story of the gradual emancipation of the industry from seignorial control does not concern us here, for it belongs to the later Middle Ages and is part of the larger story of the disintegration of the manor and the transition from medieval to modern. Indeed, the development of the cloth industry mirrors the rise and decline of the manor as it does that of the gild. Let us turn rather to consider the effects of the invention of the fulling mill and its extension in rural districts upon the old-established urban centres of the cloth industry.

The development of the fulling mill affected decisively the location of the industry, in that it determined that it should be dispersed over the countryside rather than concentrated in the towns.[60] For though at first these mills, often in remote rural valleys, dealt no doubt with the cloth woven for the needs of the rural population, ultimately they came to cater for the needs of the industrialists. Since cloth could be fulled in the mills mechanically, and therefore more cheaply, inevitably much of the work that had been done in the cities came to be sent out to them, and more and more they took over the fulling branch of the cloth industry, threatening the handcraft fullers in the towns with unemployment and starvation. In London, for instance, so serious was the competition of the country fulling mills that complaint was made to the King in 1298. It was said that certain men of the city had sent cloths "outside the city to the mill of Stratford and elsewhere,

---

[59] *Gesta Abbatam Monasterii Sancti Albani, ut supra,* I, 323, 410 *et seq.* The struggle continued, here as elsewhere, for more than a century, and was one of the causes contributing towards the Peasants' Revolt. *Cf.* the struggle at Evesham during the fourteenth and fifteenth centuries over ovens and cornmills; in 1307 a private oven erected in his house by William de Tettebury was thrown down by the Abbey steward with the aid of the town bailiffs, and in 1388 the hand mills of other tenants were destroyed, as was a horse mill in 1430. (G. May, *History of Evesham* [1845], 83.)

[60] In this respect the English industry offers a striking contrast to that of Flanders.

and caused them to be fulled there, to the grave damage of those to whom the cloth belonged and also of the men using this office in the city."[61] Round these mills grew up groups of industrial workers entirely outside the jurisdiction of urban gilds. In many little rural hamlets in valleys where water power had been turned to account we find colonies of fullers in the late thirteenth century, working evidently to supply not merely local demand. Thus there were fullers scattered throughout the West Riding valleys; at Calverley, for instance, there seem to have been at least five in about 1257.[62] The tendency for one of the chief branches of the woollen industry to shift from the town to the country gave a great stimulus to the development of the industry as a whole there, and doomed to failure the attempt of the cities to concentrate it within their walls to their own profit. To the advantages of water power were added the advantages of freedom from the high taxation in the towns and from the restrictions of the gilds. Colonies of weavers also began to settle round the fulling mills, and, as the industrial population of the rural regions increased, so that of the cities decreased, and the once mighty weavers' gilds sank into insignificance and poverty. The industry, in fact, was deserting the towns for the countryside. There is clear evidence of this decay in the case of at least seven of the leading cloth-producing cities, and others may yet be found to have been in similar case.

Winchester, for instance, in the twelfth century had a considerable number of both weavers and fullers, each organised in their own gild, and each paying £6 yearly to the crown in the time of Henry I.[63] But by the time of Edward I it was becoming increasingly difficult to collect the money, and the reason given for this was that large numbers of the clothworkers had left the town.[64] At Oxford also there was a weavers' gild paying £6 to the crown in the twelfth century.[65] But in the reign of Edward I they successfully petitioned that the sum should be reduced to 42s. on the ground that, while there used to be sixty or more weavers in the town, there were now only fifteen. Later they asked for a further reduction to 6s. 8d., since there were only seven weavers left, and those were poor; finally, in 1323, they pleaded that all these

---

[61] *Liber Custumarum, ut supra,* I, 127; *Calendar of Letter Books of the City of London; Letter Book C,* ed. R. R. Sharpe (1901), 51.

[62] H. Heaton, *The Yorkshire Woollen and Worsted Industries* (Oxford Historical and Literary Studies, X, 1920), 5, quoting *Calverley Charters,* Thoresby Society Publications, VI, 8–55.

[63] *Pipe Roll 31 Henry I,* 37.

[64] *V.C.H., Hampshire,* V (1912), 477. Complaints of financial stringency are, of course, a commonplace of the public records, but the reason here given for the difficulty, read in conjunction with the Bishop of Winchester's records, seems to bear the stamp of truth.

[65] *Pipe Roll 31 Henry I,* 2; see also *V.C.H., Oxfordshire,* II (1907), for an account of the fluctuations of the weavers' gild (242 *et seq.*).

were dead and had no successors.[66] The Lincoln weavers were also finding difficulties about paying their annual £6 to the crown in the early fourteenth century and alleged the same reasons, stating that there were no weavers left in Lincoln between 1321 and 1331 and from then until 1345 only a very few, though when Henry II granted their gild there were more than two hundred.[67] In London the number of looms was said to have fallen from 380 to 80 early in the fourteenth century.[68] York was in very similar difficulties. In the twelfth century its weavers' gild had paid a larger sum than any other—£10 annually, but during the thirteenth century it fell into more and more serious arrears, pleading in excuse that "divers men in divers places in the country, elsewhere than in the city or in the other towns and demesne boroughs—make dyed and rayed cloths."[69]

The decline of the industry in all these five boroughs is easily apparent, since each had an old-established weavers' gild, paying annually to the crown as lord of the borough. It is less easy to trace developments in the six other leading cloth-making cities, for four at least of these were not royal boroughs, none of them had privileged early gilds, so far as can be discovered, and comparable evidence is not therefore available. Yet here too we can find signs of decay. Northampton, for instance, complained in 1334 that formerly 300 clothmakers had worked there, but that now the houses where they used to live had all fallen down.[70] Leicester in 1322 declared that there was only one fuller left in the town "and he a poor man,"[71] and it is significant that from the end of the thirteenth century the very extensive Leicester records contain less and less about the cloth industry and more and more about the marketing of raw wool.

Competition from the country districts was not, of course, entirely new. Some clothmaking had always been carried on in the villages. But hitherto the "great industry" for export had been to a marked extent concentrated in the cities and controlled by them; there lived the capitalist entrepreneurs, carrying on the dyeing and finishing processes often in their own houses, and employing the colonies of skilled weavers and fullers settled within the walls, though they would also buy the rough unfinished webs brought in for sale by the country

---

[66] *Oxford Historical Society,* XXXII (1896), 99, 123–24; P.R.O. Ancient Petitions, 132/6569.

[67] *Calendar of Close Rolls, 1348–1350,* 120 (Petition of 1348); *Telariorum,* given as "spinners" in the calendar, is a synonym for *Textorum "Weavers."*

[68] Lipson, *Economic History of England, ut supra,* 450, quoting *Liber Custumarum, ut supra,* I, 416–25. Other versions give the original number as 280.

[69] Heaton, *op. cit.* 29 (Petition of 1304).

[70] *Rotuli Parliamentorum ut et Petitiones et Placita in Parliamento* (Record Commission, 1767–77), II, 85.

[71] *Calendar of Inquisitions Miscellaneous,* II, 138.

people. Now, with the invention of the fulling mill, the balance was tilted in favour of the country districts, and the cities were faced with constantly intensified competition. How then did they strive to maintain or recapture their supremacy?

Where circumstances were favourable some set up their own mills, as did Winchester in 1269, when the town granted permission to nine fullers to construct a fullers' mill.[72] But the slow-moving courses of the rivers on which most of these towns lay were less adapted to mills than were their swift upper courses, nor can the requisite space for the diversion of the watercourse have been always readily available. Moreover, there would tend to be strong opposition to an innovation which would throw so many out of work, and all the forces of conservatism would be arrayed against it.

Other towns therefore resisted the adoption of the new methods, urging the inferiority of machine work as well as the unemployment it caused. Thus a complaint from certain Londoners to the King in 1298 declared that, according to the accepted custom, cloths should be "fulled under the feet of men of this office, or their servants, in their houses in the city and not elsewhere," but that certain fullers had sent such cloths "outside the city to the mill of Stratford and elsewhere and caused them to be fulled there, to the grave damage of those to whom the cloth belonged and also of the men using this office in the city."[73] The petitioners did not, however, secure the prohibition of fulling at mills, but only an ordinance that no cloth should be sent outside the city to be fulled at mills *(pur foller as molins)* except by those who actually owned the cloth, and that six men should watch at the city gates, arrest the cloths, and keep them until the owners came and avowed them as theirs.[74] Twelve years later one Godfrey de Loveyne was heavily fined for sending three cloths outside the city to be fulled at mills.[75]

Most towns, however, concerned themselves primarily with confining the industry within the city walls. Their own civic ordinances could at least compel clothmakers in the city to employ city labour only and thus to maintain the wealth and prosperity of the city. Thus when the craft ordinances of Bristol were first written down in the city records in 1346, that of the fullers decreed *qe nul hom face amesner hors de ceste ville nule manere drap a foler qe home appele raucloth sur peyne de perdre xld. pur chescun drap.*[76] In the same ordinance

---

[72] *The Black Book of Winchester,* ed. W. H. Bird (1925), 190.

[73] *Liber Custumarum, ut supra,* I, 127.

[74] *Ibid.,* I, 127, 128; *Calendar of Letter Book C, ut supra,* 51.

[75] *Calendar of Letter Books of the City of London; Letter Book D,* ed. R. R. Sharpe (1902), 239 (*pannos crudos* is probably raw, *i.e.* unfulled, cloth, not "undyed").

[76] *Little Red Book of Bristol,* ed. F. B. Bickley (1900), II, 7.

there is mention of cloth being sent "to the mill" *(al molyn),* so that clearly the opposition was not to milling as such but to the work going out of the city. The prohibition was repeated later in the century,[77] and similar prohibitions continued to be made in other towns. At Winchester, for instance, in 1402, clothmakers of the town were forbidden to employ either fullers or weavers outside the town.[78] A somewhat similar ordinance seems to have been made at Leicester in 1260, and citizens were punished for breach of it.[79]

Such ordinances might do something to prevent city manufacturers from having dealings with workers outside, but they could not prevent an independent industry from flourishing in the country districts. Some cities therefore turned to an authority higher than that of the city and prayed the King to aid them in securing the monopoly they coveted. The York weavers, with those of other royal boroughs in Yorkshire, had already, by their charter of 1164, been granted a monopoly of making dyed and rayed cloth in all Yorkshire. At the end of the thirteenth century their monopoly was, as we have seen, being seriously infringed, so in 1304 they petitioned the King and he ordered the Exchequer to have enquiries made and to compel all found plying the craft in illegal places to refrain.[80] We do not know what effect, if any, was given to this order, but we do know that it did not, any more than did the cities' own ordinances, succeed in the impossible task of confining the cloth industry within urban walls.

The decline of the industry in the thirteenth century in what had been its most flourishing urban centres is as striking as is its expansion in rural regions during the same period, but it is the urban side of the matter which has hitherto attracted the attention of historians, and from it they have falsely deduced a decline in the industry as a whole. The real significance of this decline now becomes clear. The industry was developing, and developing rapidly, but outside the jurisdiction of those cities that had once taken the lead in it. The decay of the once famous cloth-making cities of the eastern plain and the rise of the country fulling mills shows not only that the rural industry was gaining over the urban, but also, when we consider the preponderance of fulling mills in north and west of England, that the broadcloth industry as a whole was tending to shift from east to west, to new centres in the West Riding, the Lake District and the West of England. For here were to be found ample supplies not only of fine wool but also of water power. In the twelfth and early thirteenth centuries the fine quality English cloths specially in demand abroad were cloths

---

[77] *Little Red Book of Bristol,* ed. F. B. Bickley (1900), II, 7.
[78] *Black Book of Winchester, ut supra,* 8.
[79] *Records of the Borough of Leicester, ut supra,* I, 91, 347.
[80] Heaton, *op. cit.,* 28–9.

"of Stamford," "of Lincoln," "of Louth," "of Beverley," "of York"; but in the fourteenth and fifteenth centuries there was no demand at all for these cloths, but much for "Kendals," "Ludlows," "Cotswolds," "Mendips," "Castlecombes," "Stroudwaters" or "Westerns," and the primary, though not the only, factor in this change was the invention of the fulling mill.

POSTSCRIPT

Since this article was written my attention has been called to the mention of a fulling-mill (molendino fullonario) in a charter of St. Wandrille in Normandy. This charter was dated by Ferdinand Lot at about 1086–7 (Études critiques sur l'abbaye de St. Wandrille, Bibliothéque l'École des Hautes Études, 204ᵉ fasc., Paris 1913, 96–7), but though it seems to prove that the fulling-mill had been invented by the late eleventh century it in no way invalidates the general conclusions concerning England on pages 46–47.

The development of the English woollen textile industry as a whole, from Roman to early Tudor times, was the theme of my Ford Lectures delivered at the University of Oxford in the spring of 1965 (to be published at the Clarendon Press). These lectures went more fully into the history of the industry—rural as well as urban—in the twelfth and thirteenth century, investigating in particular the crisis of the late thirteenth century. They also discussed the various factors that led to the ultimate triumph of the rural industry in the later middle ages; for though water-power was certainly one of the most important of these factors, as the article reprinted here suggests, it was not, as the article clearly indicates, the only factor.

E. M. Carus-Wilson
18 July 1967

Some Suggested Readings

Ardzrooni, Leon. "Commerce and Industry in Spain during Ancient and Medieval Times," *Journal of Political Economy*, XXI (1913), 432–53.

Brinkmann, Carl. "The Hanseatic League; A Survey of Recent Literature," *Journal of Economic and Business History*, II (1930), 585–602.

Carus-Wilson, Eleanor M. "The English Cloth Industry in the Late Twelfth and Early Thirteenth Centuries," *The Economic History Review*, XIV (1944), 32–50.

Christensen, Aksel E. "Scandinavia and the Advance of the Hanseatics," *Scandinavian Economic History Review*, V (1957), 89–117.

Werveke, Hans Van. "Industrial Growth in the Middle Ages: The Cloth Industry in Flanders," *The Economic History Review*, II (1954), 237–45.

The Medieval Roots of
Modern Technology
and Science*

Lynn T. White, Jr.

To those of us reared within the enchanted circle of Western civilization, the most treasured part of our tradition is civil rights and their juridical and parliamentary defenses. Since the days of Bishop Stubbs it has been no news that these are to a great extent dividends on the medieval legacy, although subsequent scholarship has greatly amplified and somewhat de-Anglo-Saxonized our view of such matters.

When a Syrian, a Nigerian, or a Burmese looks at the Occident, however, what does he see as really distinctive and valuable? What does he want most eagerly to appropriate for himself and his society? Generally it is not parliamentary democracy, although with the collapse of their own old regimes they have indeed taken over its external forms, *faute de mieux*. What they want are our technology and, secondarily, the natural science that we assure them is fundamental to that technology. The capacity of an industrial society to turn out goods to end the appalling poverty of the non-Western world; its ability to produce the arms that in our mad epoch are the means to a group's self-respect—these, to non-Occidentals, are the hallmarks of Westernization. Russia, beginning with Peter the Great, Japan after the Meiji Restoration, prove to them that democracy is a folkway of the West, whereas technology and science are the essence of its power.

In these papers we are dealing with the newer views of the Middle Ages and of our historical relation with them. Why bring up tech-

* Reprinted with the permission of William Marsh Rice University from *Perspectives in Medieval History*, a Rice University Semi-centennial Publication, edited by Katherine Fischer Drew and Floyd Seyward Lear and published (1963) by The University of Chicago Press, Chicago, Illinois, U.S.A.

nology and science? It has been axiomatic that the Middle Ages were an Age of Faith, which therefore must have been antipathetic toward anything legitimately called science, and that their technology was both static and negligible. The Scientific Revolution of the seventeenth century and the Industrial Revolution of the eighteenth were the antithesis of everything medieval. "God said 'Let Newton be' and all was light." As for James Watt, it never occurred to the poets that God might have had anything at all to do with him, but this attitude did not seem to reduce his effectiveness. By that time God seemed in any case a bit of a refugee from the shattered Middle Ages.

The axioms, however, are in flux. Now, and for some sixty years past, medieval science has been the subject of increasingly intensive investigation, and during the last two decades we have begun also to have a look at medieval technology, with unexpected results. Much more will be learned, but we are at a point where an intelligible new picture is emerging. What we begin to see is a continuity in the scientific and technological aspects of our culture fully comparable to that long recognized in the legal and constitutional.

Any discussion of continuity and change runs grave risks of setting up false dichotomies. Those who stress change sometimes seem to forget that it takes a river to make a waterfall, as well as a cliff for it to tumble over. Those who tend to dwell on continuity are so entranced by the river that they disregard the cliff. This sort of nonsense can best be avoided if we distinguish between *change* and *discontinuity* in cultural history. Discontinuity occurs when an item or set of items is borrowed from outside a culture and when that borrowing alters the whole style of the relevant activity in the recipient culture. Silver had been mined in Peru and copper in Katanga from very early times. Yet when in the fifteen hundreds the Spaniards brought in Europe's most skilful mining engineers to exploit the treasures of the Andes, and when the Union Minière did the same thing in Central Africa early in our own century, the styles of Andean and Congolese mining suffered such mutations that one must state the events in terms of discontinuity. On the other hand, the engineers who came to Potosí and then to Kolwezi four hundred years later, although their mining methods differed vastly, belonged to the tradition of European mining technology in which there has been much change but no discontinuity. As contrasted with discontinuity caused by borrowed elements, change that is generated internally in a tradition is powerful evidence of the continuity of that tradition.

Until recently the chronology of the Western tradition of technology has been entirely misunderstood. Even in the early Middle Ages, the parts of Europe adhering to the Latin Church began to show a technological dynamism superior to that of the generally more sophisticated cultures of Byzantium and Islam.[1]

Beginning in the sixth century, and accumulating until the end of the ninth century, an interlocking series of innovations led to a revolution in agricultural methods in northern Europe. These were the heavy plow, the open-field system, the triennial rotation of crops, a new type of harness for horses consisting of a rigid collar and lateral traces, and, finally, nailed horseshoes. Some of these may have been borrowed from Central Asia, but on the whole they seem to have been indigenous, as was their integration to form a coherent system of tillage. For climatic reasons, the new agricultural techniques were generally applicable only north of the Loire and the Alps. By the time of Charlemagne, effects of the new productivity of the northern peasants were very noticeable and, indeed, enable us to understand the shift of the focus of Europe away from the Mediterranean's shores to the great plains of the north, where it has remained ever since. By the eleventh century, the unprecedented food surpluses were reflected in a rapid increase of population. Everywhere new cities were springing up and old ones were expanding their walls to defend bursting suburbs. The tempo of manufacture, commerce, and finance, accelerated, and a new pattern of urban bourgeois life emerged.

Cultivating the soil has been, until recently, the basic human occupation. We now see that the early Middle Ages produced, in the north, a new kind of agriculture which in terms of human labor was more productive than that of any other civilized society of the time. This illuminates many problems. The stupendous capital expenditure on the Gothic cathedrals, for example, can be understood in the new economic context.

In the technology of warfare, the West likewise seized the initiative as early as the eighth century. During the 730's, there occurred a sharp discontinuity in the history of European warfare, caused by the introduction, from India by way of China, of the stirrup. The stirrup is a curious item in the history of technology because it is both cheap and easy to make, yet it makes a vast difference in what a warrior can do on a horse. As long as a man is clinging to his horse by pressure of his knees, he can wield a spear only with the strength of his arms. But when the lateral support of stirrups is added to the fore-and-aft buttressing of the pommel and cantle of a heavy saddle, horse and rider become one. Now the fighter is enabled—but not

---

[1] Save as is otherwise indicated, detailed support for the following discussion of technology may be found in my *Medieval Technology and Social Change* (Oxford, 1962). The best guide to medieval science remains G. Sarton, *Introduction to the History of Science* (3 vols. in 5; Baltimore, 1927–48) with a careful index.

required, be it noted—to lay his spear at rest between his upper arm and body. The blow is struck no longer with the strength of a man's muscles but rather by the impetus of a charging stallion and rider. The stirrup thus made possible the substitution of animal power for human power. It was the technological basis for mounted shock combat, the typical Western medieval mode of fighting.

The increase in the violence of attack was immense, and all the peoples in immediate contact with Western Christendom were compelled in self-defense to adopt the new Frankish military technology, for, as the Byzantine princess Anna Comnena ruefully admitted, "a Frank on horseback is invincible."[2] To give just one specific example of this diffusion: By about the year 1000, in order to protect the rider's left leg, the Westerners had elongated the round shield into a kite-shaped shield, pointed at the bottom. By 1066 this is found in Byzantium[3] and by 1085 in Cairo. The Spanish Muslims bitterly lamented that military exigencies had forced them to adopt the lance at rest and the heavy Christian armor and to arm their infantry with the crossbow, which they, like Anna Comnena, regarded as a Frankish novelty designed to pierce the heavy mail made necessary by shock combat.

The medieval West, then, developed not only the most productive agricultural system but also the most effective military technology of the age. The Crusades failed partly because of rivalries between the Westerners, partly because of their difficult logistic problems, but also because the Near East learned European ways of fighting. Nowhere is the admiration of the Muslim military man for the technical methods of his Frankish foes better expressed than in al-Herewī's eyewitness account of the carefully co-ordinated battle tactics, the skilful mutual support by cavalry and infantry, exhibited by the armies of the Third Crusade.

The strangest thing about this whole development is that the Franks were the last horse-riding people of Eurasia to receive the stirrup, yet they were the first to realize and exploit its full implications for warfare. There would seem to have been in the West a greater degree of openness to innovation than was to be found in the more complex and perhaps less turbulent societies of Byzantium, Islam, India, and China of that age.[4]

---

[2] *Alexiad,* trans. E. Dawes (London, 1928), p. 342.

[3] In *Medieval Technology,* p. 35, I dated the Byzantine adoption of the kite-shaped shield *ca.* 1100. For the date 1066, based on British Museum, Cod. add. 19352, fol. 87ᵛ, *cf. Late Classical and Medieval Studies in Honor of Albert Mathias Friend, Jr.,* ed. K. Weitzmann (Princeton, 1955), p. 190, Pl. XXII, 2.

[4] I have explored some reasons for this contrast in "What Accelerated Technological Progress in the Western Middle Ages?" in *Scientific Change,* ed. A. C. Crombie, to appear shortly.

The most remarkable display of technological adventuresomeness in the medieval West, however, was the elaboration of powered machines and of laborsaving devices in manufacturing. The water mill appeared in the early first century before Christ, but there is as yet no firm evidence that either water or wind power was applied to any industrial process other than grinding grain in antiquity, in Byzantium, or in Islam until very recent times. The Chinese made some progress along this line, but the Near East, like India, seems to have remained very nearly at the Roman level in the utilization of power and labor.

About the year 1000, there is a stirring in the industry of the West. A rudimentary but novel device, cams on the axle of a water wheel, is operating mechanical fulling machines in the textile industry and trip hammers for forging iron. No one has yet screened the available material, eliminating forgeries and tracing diffusions, but when that task is accomplished, our view of European economic history will be profoundly altered. By the late twelfth century, such simple machines were widespread.

The horizontal-axle windmill was invented on the shores of the North Sea shortly after 1180. An earlier vertical-axle windmill is found in southern Afghanistan, perhaps inspired by wind-driven Tibetan prayer cylinders,[5] but it was inefficient and had little diffusion even in Islam. The windmill as we know it is a Western medieval invention which vastly increased power resources in flat lands where the fall of streams was too slight for a good watermill and where a mill dam would flood too much fertile land.

About 1235 another concept emerges. Villard de Honnecourt's notebook shows the sketch of the first industrial machine to involve two correlated, fully automatic motions. It is a water-powered sawmill, which, in addition to the motion of sawing, provides an automatic feed to keep the log pressed against the saw.[6] This reflects the mentality that during the next century produced the incredibly sophisticated automation of the weight-driven mechanical clock, culminating in 1364 with the completion of Giovanni Dondi's planetarium at Pavia.[7]

The fourteenth and fifteenth centuries developed further applications of power machinery, notably powered bellows for blast furnaces and a great variety of grinding, polishing, rolling, and wiredrawing devices in the metal industries. By the end of the fifteenth century,

---

[5] See my "Tibet, India and Malaya as Sources of Western Medieval Technology," *American Historical Review,* LXV (1959–60), 515–26.

[6] *The Sketchbook of Villard de Honnecourt,* ed. T. Bowie (Bloomington, Ind., 1959), Pl. 58.

[7] Giovanni Dondi dall'Orologio, *Tractatus astrarii,* ed. A. Barzon, E. Morpurgo, A. Petrucci, and G. Francescato (Vatican City, 1960).

the cities of the more industrialized parts of Europe were filled with groups of craftsmen working, it would seem, in relatively small shops; but—in absolute contrast to the Orient—they worked habitually with machines run by natural forces and not merely by human energy.

We must reconsider what we mean by the Industrial Revolution of the eighteenth century. Its essence was not the first discovery of power machinery. Probably the core of it was the emergence of sizable factories. These were made necessary by the fact that, after seven centuries of continuous development, power machinery had reached a point of elaboration, differentiation, and expense that demanded concentration. But, clearly, this is not a historical discontinuity; it is an internally generated managerial innovation.

My fundamental proposition, then, is that the technological dominance of Western culture is not merely characteristic of the modern world: it begins to be evident in the early Middle Ages and is clear by the later Middle Ages.

It has become a platitude that the most important thing about modern technology is not inventions but rather "the invention of invention." There were inventors in antiquity, and among the Greeks in particular there was a considerable—if often mythologizing—interest in the origin of specific innovations. I have not found in antiquity, however, any indication of the idea of invention as a general enterprise looking to the future rather than as the effort to solve a particular problem. The modern notion of invention as a total movement for innovation first finds expression in a famous passage by Roger Bacon, probably written about 1260, in which he anticipates a world of motor ships, automobiles, airplanes, and submarines. Moreover, when we look at the later thirteenth century with its invention of eyeglasses and the emergence of the spinning wheel, with its records of at least two groups of men working to achieve perpetual motion, and an English cleric telling us (1271) how to build a mechanical clock, but admitting that unfortunately not all the bugs had yet been worked out of the machine, we are forced to conclude that Friar Roger was not alone in his vision of planned technical advance.

Indeed, the rapidity with which novelties spread indicates a popular receptivity to anything useful. The navigator's compass coming from China—across Central Asia and not through Islam, it would seem—reached the West at the very end of the twelfth century. By 1218 Jacques de Vitry considered it essential to any sailing on the sea, and seven years later it was already in habitual use in Iceland. Yet no Muslim reference to the compass has been found earlier than 1232–33, which would seem to indicate less receptivity in Islam. An even more spectacular example of speedy diffusion is the windmill. The earliest one firmly dated is found in Yorkshire in 1185, yet seven years later German Crusaders had built the first ever seen in Syria. Within a few decades, it had become a normal part of most European landscapes. When about 1322, an English chronicler can credit the deforestation of England in part to the search for the long beams needed for windmill vanes,[8] we are obviously dealing with an age eagerly exploiting mechanical power.

There is a persistent opinion that before the Industrial Revolution there was widespread opposition to technological changes, particularly on the part of the guilds. The vernacular presentation of this topic cites Suetonius' story of how Vespasian declined to use a laborsaving hoist because it would cause unemployment among the Roman rabble, goes on to the (entirely ineffective) prohibition by the Second Lateran Council in 1139 of the use of the crossbow when fighting fellow Christians, and generally ends with early modern textile workers smashing stocking-knitting machines. We must eventually remedy this sort of rampaging down through the ages. We still lack a firmly constructed history of attitudes toward technological change. As a result of desultory rummagings, I believe at present that in the Middle Ages there was no opposition to any novelty that seemed to those closest to the matter to be profitable. The clergy of the twelfth century might indeed ban the crossbow and two hundred years later might shake benign tonsured pates over the satanic qualities of gunpowder; but the men whose business it was to use weapons used the most effective weapons they could get. The guilds were made up of canny craftsmen interested in efficient production and quite aware that, if they failed to adopt a good new gadget, their export trade would quickly lose markets to the guild in the next city that had permitted its use. Indeed, technological change often caused great disruption of industry yet was not opposed. In a classic study E. M. Carus-Wilson[9] has shown that in thirteenth-century England the displacement of hand-fulling by mechanical fulling led to the shift of the center of English textile manufacturing from the southeast part of the island to the more accidented northwest, where water-power sites were more readily available. When the spinning wheel first appeared in Europe toward the end of the thirteenth century, it must have caused unemployment among those who provided commercial yarn for the weavers. Yet the first mention of the spinning wheel, in a guild regulation in Speyer, *ca.* 1280, does not forbid it but merely prohibits the use of wheel-spun thread in the warp (as distinct from the weft), presumably because it was not yet as strong as that produced in the old way. The object, then, was to protect the quality of cloth.

---

[8] W. Dugdale, *Monasticon anglicanum* (2d ed.; London, 1682), I, 816.

[9] "An Industrial Revolution of the Thirteenth Century," *The Economic History Review,* XI (1941), 39–60; cf. *ibid.,* 2d ser., III (1950–51), 342–43.

It is my impression that very little guild opposition to industrial changes can be found before the sixteenth century and that when at last it appeared it was because the pace of technological advance had become so rapid that a new industrial system was appearing, the guild structure was slipping, and the guilds were fighting for their existence.

Fighting in vain, one must add. The only case in which, as far as I know, a guild succeeded in holding back technical progress for any considerable time was a victory due to entirely exceptional circumstances. In 1534, an Italian, Matteo del Nassaro, built a mill on piles over the Seine at Paris to polish precious stones for jewelry. In 1552 this was bought by the royal mint and equipped with new water-powered machines recently designed at Augsburg to produce coins. In 1559 King Henry II died, and the guild of coiners persuaded the advisers of his sixteen-year-old successor, Francis II, to abandon the enterprise and restrict the use of power machines to the production of medals. Thenceforth in France coins were "struck" in the traditional way until 1645.[10] It is clear, however, that if the guild of coiners had not been dealing with a rigorously enforced royal monopoly of coinage, if they had been in a typical competitive market, their efforts to block innovation would have crumbled quickly, as other such attempts did. As long as the guilds were a flourishing part of medieval society, they were strong enough to accept technological change. Only when the guild structure became senile, because it had lost touch with the new economic order, did the guilds try to block change.

Thus far I have scarcely mentioned medieval science. In the twentieth century, science-and-technology is a hyphenated word, and science has priority in our minds. We think of technology as being applied science.

The situation in the Middle Ages was entirely different. From what I have said, it is clear that the supremacy of the Occident in technology antedates by several centuries its pre-eminence in science. Moreover, technological achievements and problems cannot be shown to have had much direct influence on the growth of medieval science, and scientific discoveries did not affect the growth of technology.

The history of European technology, from the earliest times to the present, is one of constant change but of no discontinuity as a whole, even at the time of the collapse of the Western Roman Empire. The only striking discontinuity in a single area of technology was that in the art of war in the eighth century brought about by the arrival of the stirrup. Even the development of gunpowder artillery in the early fourteenth century brought no such rapid shift in the style of combat, and in any case cannon may have been indigenous to Europe.

---

[10] A. Blanchet and A. Dieudonné, *Manuel de numismatique française* (Paris, 1916), II, 192–93.

The history of Occidental science, on the other hand, has a much more irregular pattern. There is nothing in the early Western Middle Ages that we would wish to call "science." The Romans were remarkably indifferent to the achievements of Greek science and translated few of the Greek texts into Latin.[11] When knowledge of the Greek tongue decayed in the West, science dropped below its eastern horizon. About the year 1000, Gerbert of Aurillac (Pope Sylvester II), the liveliest scholar of his time in the Latin world, was interested in science and did his best.[12] His actual knowledge of science, however, was pathetic.

The scientific movement in the West, of which we today are the direct heirs, started with a seismic discontinuity in the later eleventh century—a complete break with the past and the borrowing en masse from Byzantium and Islam of ancient Greek science and of the contemporary Arabic science that had been elaborated on Greek and Indic foundations. The suddenness and avidity with which the West turned to an alien science demands explanation, but I shall not attempt it here.[13] Suffice it to say that within about two hundred years, that is, roughly from the first translations of Constantine the African about 1060 to the death of William of Moerbeke in 1286, the great bulk of Greek and Muslim science was made available in Latin and was rather well assimilated by the West.

From the later thirteenth century onward, Occidentals began making significant original scientific discoveries, as, for example, in Peter of Maricourt's pioneering study (1269) of magnetism. To be sure, the pre-eminence of late medieval science is partly a matter of lack of competition. Byzantium, which in any case had been scholarly rather than experimental in science, was declining under Turkish assault. Islam, after nearly four centuries of brilliant scientific achievements, had begun after 1100 to turn from the study of external facts to the contemplation of the inner fact of the soul,[14] and her scientific

---

[11] The excellent study by W. H. Stahl, *Roman Science* (Madison, Wis., 1962), p. 251, asserts that "most of the manifestations of low-level scientific and philosophical thinking that we associate with the Dark Ages appear among the Romans."

[12] One of the earliest indications of versions of Arabic science in Latin appears in Gerbert's letter of 984 to Lupitus of Barcelona asking for an astronomical treatise that the latter had translated; *cf. The Letters of Gerbert,* trans. H. P. Lattin (New York, 1961), p. 69.

[13] For some aspects of the problem, see my "Natural Science and Naturalistic Art in the Middle Ages," *American Historical Review,* LII (1946–47), 421–35.

[14] W. Hartner, "Quand et comment s'est arrêté l'essor de la culture scientifique dans l'Islam?" in *Classicisme et declin culturel dans l'histoire de l'Islam,* ed. R. Brunschvig and G. E. von Grunebaum (Paris, 1957), pp. 318–37, should be read in the context of the extraordinary essay by G. E. von Grunebaum,

vigor waned rapidly. Nevertheless, Western science in the fourteenth and fifteenth centuries has both great inherent interest and high significance for the so-called Scientific Revolution that built upon it.

Late medieval science put little stress on experiment. It was "natural philosophy," highly speculative and often mathematical: for example, early in the fourteenth century, trigonometry spurted ahead in the work of clergy at Merton College, Oxford, and of the Provencal Jew Levi ben Gerson. Both the limitations and the great originality of European science at that time must be understood in the context of the intellectual crises of the period.[15] Conservative theologians were horrified by the implication of Thomas Aquinas' effort to incorporate Aristotelian philosophy into the Christian intellectual system and to make it a rational means of validating what they regarded as revealed truths. To defend their neo-Augustinian position, they launched a savage and brilliant counterattack upon Aristotle, designed to distinguish sharply between the sorts of knowledge that are accessible to human faculties and the sorts of knowledge that can be got only by revelation. In the process, they pushed the whole of metaphysics into the area of revelation. Thus they destroyed the entire prior Greek and Muslim concept of the metaphysical nature of the philosophical venture and invented the empirical, that is, the modern, notion of what philosophy is all about. The crisis of the fourteenth century is thus the most creative moment in the history of Western thought.

It was inherent in the nature of this intellectual revolution that philosophy, which hitherto had been oriented toward theology, should now become reoriented toward science, as it still is. Aristotle's qualitative-metaphysical physics was assaulted by means of a new quantitative-empirical physics. By daring and ingenious analysis, for example, it was shown that Aristotle's theory of moving bodies was false, and a new theory of motion was propounded which is essentially that of Galileo or Newton.[16]

Unfortunately, the scholastic scientists thought that if they had proved a point logically, they had proved it. Some generations passed before it was widely felt necessary to supplement pure thought by rolling balls down inclined planes or dropping weights from towers and timing the fall. The Scientific Revolution of the seventeenth century was in every sense the child of late medieval science, although a

---

"The World of Islam: The Face of the Antagonist," in *Twelfth-Century Europe and the Foundations of Modern Society,* ed. M. Clagett, G. Post, and R. Reynolds (Madison, Wis., 1961), pp. 189–211.

[15] Best depicted by E. A. Moody, "Empiricism and Metaphysics in Medieval Philosophy," *Philosophical Review,* LXVII (1958), 145–63.

[16] For the continuity of the discussion of motion between the fourteenth and the seventeenth centuries, see M. Clagett, *The Science of Mechanics in the Middle Ages* (Madison, Wis., 1959), pp. 629–71.

rebellious child. There grew up discontent with speculative science, a realization of the necessity for experiment, and an instinct for the working hypothesis as a guide to experiment. Here we observe great change, but no discontinuity.

There is, however, another significant element in the build-up for the age of Kepler, Descartes, and Newton: the successes of medieval technology. I have not found any instance during the Middle Ages of a scientific discovery that resulted in technological innovation. Indeed, I doubt whether any such case can be established before Von Guericke's and Papin's investigation of vacua and pressures clarified the problem of harnessing steam power. There is, however, a flow of ideas and stimuli from technology to science in the earlier period.

In one medieval case, a scientific *need,* not a discovery, resulted in technological advance. Astronomers found water clocks unsatisfactory because on cold nights the outlets became coated with ice and the timing of observations was inaccurate. Mercury could be substituted for water, but it was costly. Sand abraded the aperture through which it flowed, and in any case there is no sign of a sandglass much earlier than the mechanical clock. Obviously, a weight-driven clock was needed. For perhaps seventy years, astronomers and mechanics struggled to devise one. At last, shortly before the 1340's, they succeeded, and within a few decades Europe was filled with mechanical clocks of astonishing elaboration. The building and repair of them and the rapid emergence of a large clock- and watch-making industry established the basis for providing the exact mechanical apparatus of subsequent scientific investigation. The greatest single need at the present time in the history of science is a rigorous and detailed history of instrumentation.[17] It would show, I suspect, that lags in science have often been related to a dearth of technical means for securing information and that scientific advance has often attended a technological breakthrough.

Such a study might also explain puzzling delays in the development of scientific apparatus long after craftsmen had made their elements available. In the Museum of the History of Science in Florence, one may view Galileo's telescope, which transformed Copernicus' mathematical-speculative, late medieval astronomical system into modern observational Copernicanism. One genuflects before the memory of Galileo; but then one wonders why that telescope had not been invented three centuries earlier.

---

[17] A. Rohde, *Die Geschichte der wissenschaftliche Instrumente vom Beginn der Renaissance bis zum Ausgang des 18. Jahrhunderts* (Leipzig, 1923), and G. Boffito, *Gli strumenti della scienza e la scienza degli strumenti* (Florence, 1929), are outdated. M. Daumas, *Les instruments scientifiques aux XVIIe et XVIIIe siècles* (Paris, 1953) is excellent for the period covered.

Certainly if someone like John Buridan had used a telescope, we could not be astonished. By the fourteenth century, the study of theoretical optics had reached a remarkable state, providing, for example, sophisticated explanations of the rainbow. Moreover, in the thirteenth century, lenses and their magnifying properties came to be known. Fra Salimbene tells us that when the relics of St. Mary Magdalene were found in Provence in 1283 a parchment was found with them which "vix potuit legi . . . cum cristallo propter scripture antiquitatem."[18] A friend of Bacon made a lens with great effort, which Bacon sent as a gift to the pope. Moreover, Bacon knew, as did Robert Grosseteste, that lenses placed in a series increase magnification. Doubtless the earliest thirteenth-century lenses were made of rock crystal, but toward the end of the century, the Italian glass industry learned how to produce a clear and colorless glass like crystal.[19] At that same moment, methods of cutting rock crystal and gems were greatly improved,[20] and these advances assisted the grinding of good lenses from glass as well. In the late 1280's, a man who lived along the lower Arno, probably in Pisa or Lucca, invented eyeglasses. We do not know his name, but there is an explicit and convincing reference to him in a sermon preached in Florence a few years later.[21] In Europe the use of eyeglasses quickly became normal; thence they spread over Eurasia: about 1480 the Persian poet Jāmī still speaks of eyeglasses as "Frankish."[22]

In these circumstances, why didn't the fourteenth century have the telescope? I do not know. All that can be said at present is that when at last a contemporary of Galileo did achieve it, he was resting his invention on the work of late-thirteenth-century glass-makers and gem-cutters.

Instrumentation, then, was one of the ways in which medieval technology aided the scientific movement. In another way, technology gave scientists new problems to think about. As we have seen, the mariner's compass was a novelty in the thirteenth century. Peter of Maricourt's *Epistola de magnete* would seem to have been inspired by watching compass-makers at work, possibly at the port of Amalfi, because we know that he wrote it to relieve boredom at the lengthy siege of Lucera in 1269, where he was serving Charles of Anjou as a

---

[18] *Cronica,* ed. O. Holder-Egger (Hanover, 1905–13), p. 520.

[19] A. Gasparetto, *Il vetro di Murano* (Venice, 1958), pp. 59–61.

[20] H. R. Hahnloser, "Scola et artes cristellariorum de Veneciis, 1284–1319," in *Venezia e l'Europa, Atti del XVIII Congresso Internazionale di Storia dell'Arte* (Venice, 1956), pp. 157–65.

[21] E. Rosen, "The Invention of Eyeglasses," *Journal of the History of Medicine and Allied Sciences,* XI (1956), 13–46.

[22] A. J. Arberry, *Classical Persian Literature* (London, 1958), p. 440. I owe this reference to my colleague Gustave von Grunebaum.

71

military engineer. His treatise is today recognized as the cornerstone of William Gilbert's *De magnete* (1600) and therefore of our entire knowledge of magnetism.

Another stimulus to science came from ballistics. It has often been pointed out that Galileo was intensely interested in the activities at the arsenal of Venice, and some have gone so far as to assert that seventeenth-century physics was born of such technological concerns. This is an oversimplification, because it disregards the continuity of early modern physics with that of the fourteenth century. Late medieval physicists were entirely conscious that the projectiles of trebuchets and cannon involved the theory of moving bodies, and they occasionally refer to them. The seventeenth-century emphasis on the importance of observation and experiment simply brought physics closer to the phenomena provided by artillery, to the eventual advance of both science and technology.

One of my students, Sheldon Shapiro, has recently turned up a particularly elegant and clear case in which a mechanical device posed to science a basic theoretical problem. He has pointed out for the first time that the suction pump was invented in Italy somewhat before the middle of the fifteenth century. The suction pump enabled Galileo to observe that a column of water breaks at about thirty-two feet, and it is difficult to imagine other circumstances, save the siphon, in which anyone could have noticed this phenomenon. I need not elaborate here the vast implications of the study of vacua and atmospheric pressures that eventuated.

During the Middle Ages, then, and indeed into the seventeenth century, insofar as science and technology were related, influences passed from technology to science much more powerfully than from science to technology. When does the direction of flow change and the modern dependence of technology upon scientific discovery develop? In industrial chemistry, there are signs of it at the end of the eighteenth century, but one must recall that Pasteur's greatest insights stemmed from technical problems like those of the brewing industry. The industrial laboratory with any initial concern for basic scientific discoveries that it is hoped may possibly have application is a creation of the early twentieth century. If one regards this change in the connection between science and technology as the primary event of modern history, then the Middle Ages extend to the death of the Good Queen, the Albert Memorial becomes authentic Gothic, and Rudyard Kipling is the last of the Crusaders—a tenable hypothesis!

The essential relationship between science and technology in the Middle Ages, however, may be deeper than any we have mentioned. The agricultural revolution of the early Middle Ages made possible rapid urbanization. The new bourgeois groups quickly applied water-

and wind-power to production. The result was a prosperous, adventurous Europe, much interested in physical and earthly matters and firmly convinced of the Christian doctrine that the world was created for man's benefit and that he has a spiritual responsibility to master it. Medieval technology was therefore instrumental in evoking and supporting a society with attitudes congenial to the effort to understand natural phenomena. The feverish appropriation of Greek and Arabic science from the eleventh through the thirteenth centuries can best be understood in such terms.

Let me add a coda. Thus far I have not used the word "Renaissance." In the history of literature, the fine arts, and philosophy—at least the history of the Platonic philosophy, which for a time attempted to revive metaphysics—the concept of a classical Renaissance starting in Italy and spreading in widening circles appears to be indispensable. It may have some validity also for political theory, but for the history of practical politics, economics, and social change it seems irrelevant, save as individuals and groups strove to find status by embellishing themselves with classical ornament. In the history of science and technology, I do not find the idea of a Renaissance useful for interpreting the facts.

As is now recognized, the chief period of Europe's reappropriation of Greek science extends from the later eleventh century through the thirteenth century and marks the birth of our present scientific movement. During the later fifteenth and the sixteenth centuries, the revival of Greek studies in the West led to the recovery of some Greek scientific writings that had escaped medieval translation and to the editing of the far larger mass of Greek texts that had long been known in translations of varying merit. The scholarly interest of such publication was great, but what was the scientific increment of all this philological activity? Historians, just because their trade leads them to enjoy original texts carefully edited, have generally been deceived in this matter. The most significant of the works newly recovered in the sixteenth century were those of Archimedes, the substance of which had been only partly known through later Greek and Arabic treatises. The new Archimedes greatly stimulated both mathematics and physics. The fact that it was published in 1543, the year that likewise saw the appearance of Copernicus' work and of Vesalius' *Fabrica,* indicates, however, that it was in no way decisive for the European scientific movement. By the later fifteenth and sixteenth centuries—a period when for the first time the West was dazzled by the vision of Greek poetry, drama, history, and art—Europe's science had relatively little to learn from antiquity: five centuries of assimilation were reaching the end of their work.

The case is even clearer in technology. Vitruvius was not widely read in the Middle Ages because the men who built Cluny and Beauvais did not need him. He had tremendous vogue in the Renaissance not for his engineering but for his esthetics: he enabled architects to recover the canons of the Roman style and helped to validate the revolt against the Gothic.

In the sixteenth century, Hero of Alexandria's works were recovered and edited. The Western Middle Ages had not translated them, any more than they had Latinized al-Jazarī's Arabic book on automata (A.D. 1205), which in Islam was so highly regarded that it went into Persian and (probably) Turkish versions. The reason would seem to be that by the thirteenth century Western technicians were already exploring more advanced mechanical forms of automation than are found in the Hellenistic and Muslim treatises. The cock, crowing and flapping its wings, that by 1354 was crowning the great clock of Strasbourg was structurally much more complex than anything described in the classical or oriental works. Even after the publication of Hero's writings, the automata of the later Renaissance and Baroque generally followed the medieval mechanical tradition rather than the hydraulic and pneumatic precedents of earlier technologies.

During the fifteenth and sixteenth centuries, Italy, and to a slightly less extent the north as well, was seething with technological innovation. I have examined several of the still unpublished manuscripts of engineers of this period and find in them an excitement, an originality, and a significance for the origins of the modern world that make them as fascinating as anything that contemporary art or literature can offer. But, whereas the architectural sketches in these notebooks are invariably classicizing, I see no trace in them of recovered items of ancient engineering, save the hodometer, nor can I suggest what else of use there was to have been recovered. The classical Renaissance, which in some areas of life was an inundating wave, created scarcely a ripple in technology. Despite many incidental borrowings, especially from China, the technological tradition of the Occident, which achieved its dynamism in the early Middle Ages, has been subject to few strong external influences. It has moved under its own impetus of creativity from its origins to our own day.

Some Suggested Readings

Dempsey, Bernard M. "Just Price in a Functional Economy," *American Economic Review*, XXV (1935), 471–86.

Dowd, Douglas F. "The Economic Expansion of Lombardy, 1300–1500: A Study in Political Stimuli to Economic Change," *Journal of Economic History*, XXI (1961), 143–60.

Reynolds, Robert L. "Origins of Modern Business Enterprise: Medieval Italy," *Journal of Economic History,* XII (1952), 350–65.

Strieder, Jacob. "Origin and Evolution of Early European Capitalism," *Journal of Economic and Business History,* II (1929), 1–19.

White, Lynn Jr., "Technology and Invention in the Middle Ages," *Speculum,* XV (1940), 141–56.

English Craft Gilds in the Middle Ages*

Eileen E. Power

It was of the essence of the gild system[1] in its ideal that every master craftsman was at once capitalist and worker, manufacturer and merchant; he bought, or received from his customers, his own raw material, and sold in his own workshop the finished product of his labour. It was of the essence of the gild system, also, that there was no such thing as a permanent wage-earning class; the apprentice who had trained for seven years under a master was himself qualified to set up as a master. He might have to work for a few years as a journeyman for wages, in order to accumulate a little capital on which to set up shop, but he had no thought of remaining permanently as a servant hired at a wage. Further, it was of the essence of the gild system that the affairs of each craft, comprising prices, work-

---

* Reprinted from *History*, New Ser., Vol. IV (1919–20), by permission of the publisher.

[1] The best introduction to English craft gilds is E. Lipson, *Economic History of England* (1915), ch. viii. The best introduction to craft gilds in general, concerned mainly with Continental crafts, is a recently published translation of part of a larger work by Georges Renard, *Gilds in the Middle Ages, translated by Dorothy Terry and edited with an introduction by G. D. H. Cole* (Bell, 1919), which is very convenient and cheap; Gild Socialists are usually somewhat wild in their references to history, but Mr. Cole's introduction is moderate and suggestive. Good chapters on English crafts are to be found in W. J. Ashley, *Introduction to English Economic History*, Part I. (1888), ch. ii.; Part II. (1893), chh. i–iii.; and W. Cunningham, *Growth of English Industry and Commerce (Early and Middle Ages)* (1910 edition). J. M. Lambert, *Two Thousand Years of Gild Life* (1891), is mainly a study of the gilds of Kingston-upon-Hull, useful for its reprints of gild regulations. Regulations of many craft gilds are printed in *English Gilds, ed. Toulmin Smith, with an introduction by L. Brentano (Early English Text Soc., 1892)*, but Brentano's introduction has been superseded by later works. The best, almost the only, work on the gilds of the sixteenth and seventeenth century is G. Unwin, *Industrial Organisation in the Sixteenth and Seventeenth Centuries* (1904). See also his valuable *The Gilds and Companies of London* (1908) for London gilds throughout their history.

76

manship, and the standard of life of the workers, were regulated by the whole body of masters, working through officials. It was in its ideal a perfect industrial democracy.

The obvious advantages of this system have caused a wholesale idealisation of the middle ages by many modern writers, and in particular by those romantic socialists who followed William Morris, and by their less romantic successors, the Gild Socialists, who follow Mr. G. D. H. Cole. Now Gild Socialism is an exceedingly interesting theory, and will stand or fall upon its own merits; in any case, the fact that it envisages national and not municipal gilds, and industrial and not craft organisation, makes it essentially different from the craft gilds of the middle ages. But in their enthusiasm for the gild idea modern reformers have not infrequently delivered themselves of rash generalisations about history, which are in need of correction. The average socialist and the man in the street are apt to regard the gild system as one which flourished widely and with excellent results in England, for a halcyon period of nearly three centuries in the middle ages, at the close of which period it abruptly broke down. Their explanation of its disappearance is exceedingly simple. "In Western Europe," says Mr. Arthur Penty, the real inventor of Gild Socialism, "the gilds existed until the close of the middle ages. They fell before the economic and political upheavals which accompanied the discovery of America and the sea route to Asia, which involved as a natural consequence the change of trade routes and the growth of capitalism."[2] The artificial simplicity of such an explanation is enough to make any historian doubt it at once, and, indeed, it bears singularly little relation to the real history of the decline of the gilds.

There are two mistakes in the popular view: (1) It is far too sweeping a generalisation, and (2) it considerably post-dates the appearance of capitalism. It is true that gilds were found in many English towns from the thirteenth century onwards, but there never was so to speak, a *gild period;* that is to say, a period at which the gild system of organisation was in full working order all over the country. No century can be pointed out as the century in which the gilds everywhere flourished, no century as that in which they everywhere decayed. The only generalisation which can ever be safely made in mediæval economic history is that no generalisation can be made; all development is local, and the solution of most of the vexed questions of agrarian and industrial organisation and of many strange divergencies of evidence lies in this fact. The development of the

---

[2] A. J. Penty. *Old Worlds for New* (1917), pp. 44–45. An even more grotesque account of the appearance of capitalism and the disappearance of a mythical "distributive" State is given by Mr. Hilaire Belloc in *The Servile State* (1912).

English craft gilds varies not only from time to time (which is the only variation allowed by the average person), but from town to town, and even from craft to craft. At one and the same moment one town will have no craft gilds at all, a second will have craft gilds in full working order, a third will have strikes and unions of wage-earners. At one and the same moment in the same town one craft will be a perfect little industrial democracy, and another will be a seething struggle of labour against capital.

In some towns craft gilds appear very early. London seems never to have gone through the preliminary stage of a general Gild Merchant for the regulation of both industry and trade; and in most of the important trading centres, such as Bristol, York and Coventry, the Gild Merchant was superseded by the crafts at an early date. But in other towns craft gilds only developed quite late in their history, and in some there were never a sufficient number of workers in the different occupations to necessitate separate organisations; in such towns the old gild merchant, or the general governing body of the town, sufficed throughout the middle ages to supervise industry. At Cambridge, for instance, in spite of the demands of the University upon industry, no craft gilds ever existed; and several great modern centres, such as Manchester, Birmingham, and Sheffield, remained mere agricultural villages without crafts all through the middle ages. Thus craft gilds were at no period universal in English towns.

On the other hand, the appearance of capitalism must not be post-dated. It is true that both trade and capitalism received a great impetus with the discovery of new routes and markets at the close of the middle ages; but that impetus only hastened a process which had begun long before. The fourteenth century showed a very advanced state of capitalism in certain towns and in certain trades. The market for goods was growing steadily all through the later middle ages, and a wide market always brings with it a capitalist. Thus, though in smaller towns and crafts the gild system might be working very well in the fourteenth century, in larger industrial centres and in the more important crafts it had begun to break down. It depends essentially upon a small and stable market, a *town* market, in which the master craftsman can be his own merchant and need not depend upon a middleman to distribute his goods. It depends also upon an approximate equality of wealth among masters. But these conditions no longer existed in London and in the larger towns in the fourteenth century. The market had grown wide, and certain men had grown rich. It became increasingly difficult for the small master to distribute his goods over a wide market, and the richer masters began to specialise in distribution, rather than in production, thereby growing richer still. Under the name of the *Livery* they monopolised the government of the craft, which became an oligarchy, instead of a democracy. In order to raise profits by diminishing competition, they entered upon a narrow and restrictive policy of keeping would-be apprentices out of the gilds, by high entrance fees and a variety of other devices. It is possible that craft gilds, even at their height, did not contain all the workers in any industry, but now a great and increasing mass of labour was outside the gild system. Many boys remained outside as skilled labourers, but many were employed in the workshops of masters as "serving men," who, although never apprenticed, must for all that have been skilled. It seems probable that many of these "yeomen," or "serving men," of whom we hear in the fourteenth and fifteenth centuries, were not *journeymen,* in its gild meaning of fully trained apprentices working for a wage. Moreover, the capitalist masters not only made it difficult for boys to be apprenticed; they also made it difficult for fully trained apprentices to set up shops of their own, by making the mastership an expensive privilege. Thus many journeymen had to hire themselves out permanently at a wage, and what was meant to be a mere stage in their career became a permanent condition. The result was that already in the fourteenth century, in large towns and in important industries, there was a fully-established wages system and an acute divergence between capital and labour going on side by side with the gild system. The journeymen protected their interests as best they might, by forming associations of their own (yeoman gilds), to keep up wages, and by organising strikes; and the unapprenticed serving men seem to have made common cause with them. All this took place, not at the close of the middle ages, but in the very heart of the fourteenth century.

Similarly it seems probable that the outwork system, by which workers work in their own homes for a capitalist entrepreneur, was beginning to gain ground in industry long before the sixteenth century, when it became prominent. The untrained "serving men" probably began at quite an early date to accept work in their own homes for the richer of the shop-keeping masters; and the more these rich masters specialised in distribution, the more likely they were to give out work to be done in this way, and even to take work done by smaller masters, who found it impossible to sell their own wares in the face of the competition of the large shops. We see this happening quite clearly in the early sixteenth century, and it was a well-established practice by that time. Moreover, in the fourteenth century, there began in large towns the tendency for separate crafts to amalgamate, and for the lesser handicrafts to become absorbed into a mercantile craft. Thus in the fourteenth century the London pursers, pouchers, and glovers seem to have worked primarily not for the public, but for the leathersellers; all are separate crafts with separate gild organisations, but one craft acts as a middleman to the others. By the sixteenth century the leathersellers have completely swallowed up the three lesser handicrafts, which no longer have a separate organisation, but are organised as a dependent branch *(Yeomanry)* of the Leathersellers' Company; the individual purser, poucher, or glover is now working on an outwork system for a capitalist middleman.

The net result is that in the fourteenth century, and possibly earlier, the market was wide enough and capitalism sufficiently developed to have broken up the gild system in the larger towns and industries, which were affected by the wider markets. In these a wages system and an "outwork" organisation had appeared. In smaller towns and crafts the gild system still flourished. It is unfortunate that we know much more about the decaying gilds of London and the large towns, than we do about conditions in smaller places, though this fact makes the rash generalisations of the man in the street all the more surprising. A great deal of very careful research is still needed as to—(1) the prevalence of craft gilds in the smaller English towns; (2) the question whether at any time the craft gilds in any particular town contained the whole or the greater number of the workers in the occupations so organised: it seems probable that they did not; (3) the process by which the gild organisation declined. Professor Unwin has given us excellent studies of the process in London, but a great deal of work has yet to be done among the records of other towns in the fifteenth and sixteenth centuries. Meanwhile it is wise not to be too glib about the gild system in the middle ages.

Some Suggested Readings

Cunningham, William. "The Gild Merchant in England," *Quarterly Journal of Economics,* V (1891), 339–53.

Knoop, Douglas, and Jones, G. P. "Masons and Apprenticeship in Medieval England," *The Economic History Review,* III (1932), 346–66.

Stephenson, Carl. "In Praise of Medieval Tinkers," *Journal of Economic History,* VIII (1948), 26–42.

Thrupp, Sylvia L. "Medieval Gilds Reconsidered," *Journal of Economic History,* II (1942), 164–73.

Thrupp, Sylvia L. "Social Control in the Medieval Town," *Journal of Economic History,* I (1941), 39–52.

The Origins of Banking: The Primitive Bank of Deposit, 1200-1600*

Abbott Payson Usher

I

The study of the origins and early history of banking[1] raises a broad problem of definition. What is the simplest credit agency that can legitimately be called a bank? It is clearly important to draw some distinction between isolated credit transactions and organized banking. The lending of coined money, with or without interest, merely transfers purchasing power from one person to another. The mere acceptance of deposits of coined money involves no banking activity, even if the money is used in trade. In such a case, too, there is merely a transfer of purchasing power. Banking begins only when

* Reprinted from *The Economic History Review,* Vol. IV (1934), by permission of the publisher.

[1] The source materials from Barcelona upon which the present study is largely based were collected in 1929. Travelling expenses and the costs of more than two thousand photostats were covered by grants made by the Committee on the Milton Fund of Harvard University, and by the Committee of the Social Science Research Council on Grants in Aid. These original grants also covered the costs of clerical expenses involved in preparing translations of about one-third of the material. The Committee on Research in the Social Sciences has assisted, in the years 1932–33, and 1933–34, with grants to meet certain clerical expenses of work upon these materials and the published sources available for the study of banking in Italy. Careful study of these Italian and Catalan sources shows clearly that the Catalan material must be regarded as the controlling source for the period prior to 1500. The material at Barcelona is more abundant and more varied in character than for any single region in Italy. In Sicily, relatively few ordinances are available prior to 1500. At Venice, there are ordinances, but no accounts or business documents. The lack of accounts is serious. Printed inventories for Italy contain no indication of additional bank accounts prior to 1500, except at Genoa. These Genoese accounts seem to be the only known material prior to 1500, not already utilized or published *in*

loans are made in bank credit. This is possible only when deposits nominally payable in specie on demand can be used effectively by a system of book transfer and clearance. The banker can then use some of the deposits to make loans or engage in trade without depriving the depositors of the free use of their deposits. The deposits become a means of payment that is independent of specie to the extent that the transactions involved can be offset by book clearance without using specie. Deposits thus become bank money, and are consciously recognized as an independent means of payment as early as the fifteenth century. In Venice, an ordinance of 1421 uses the expression *contadi di banco,* in antithesis to *denari contadi.*[2] These phrases can be adequately rendered only as "bank money" and "cash." The phrase "payment in bank," or its equivalent, appears at least as early both in Barcelona and in Sicily. These expressions indicate a somewhat tardy recognition of the essential character of banking, and the effective practice of banking must be recognized as having been already long established.

Although the lending of credit is the essential function of the banker, it is not always possible to secure specific evidence as to the nature of loans in the early historical period, and for purposes of historical criticism it is best to use more objective tests. The lending of credit becomes an assured possibility as soon as a considerable number of current deposit accounts can be drawn together in one enterprise. We may therefore presume that banking begins when we are able to find separate accounting units handling some appreciable number of current accounts. Even if the proprietors of the business are engaged in other affairs, we are entitled to speak of a bank if a separate set of books is kept for the banking business.

In studying the twelfth and thirteenth centuries, practical historical problems require us to distinguish banking from dealings in domestic and foreign coin or from the casual credit transactions that would necessarily appear in any mercantile business. Money-changing involved no use of credit in any form, and though some of the money-changers

---

extenso. The records at Barcelona contain a large number of ordinances, many registers of accounts for the critical period 1370–1450, and large masses of business documents. Additional material is available at Valencia. The Italian material becomes much more abundant after 1500, but new interests are involved. The development of the cheque and of the doctrine of negotiability dominates the period 1500–1700. Failure to recognize the extent of these changes has led to many errors in the interpretation of the earlier documents. The present paper is a preliminary statement of the general conclusions that have emerged from an intensive study of these materials. The work is now far advanced, but the preparation of the full text is a laborious task that will require no little time.

[2] Lattes, E., *La liberta delle banche a Venezia dal secolo XIII al XVII,* p. 47, Milano, 1869.

became bankers, the enlargement of function was usually recognized by some distinguishing qualification. In Catalonia, the bankers were called bonded money-changers, or public money-changers. Dealers in coin were called petty money-changers. In many parts of Italy the term "banker" appears at an early date, but, unfortunately, without assured accuracy in usage. These terms are, thus, a peculiarly unsatisfactory basis for the establishment of the beginnings of banking. Whenever it can be established that these money-changers or bankers are actually holding deposits on current account we may safely presume that the characteristic banking functions are being exercised.

Merchants were inevitably engaged in various credit transactions. Many of them were involved in various partnerships for particular ventures or for the activities of a continuing enterprise. If the funds were furnished by a silent partner, they were, in a sense, deposited with the active partner for use in trade. Such deposits were not sharply distinguished in contemporary law from the deposits held by bankers on current account, but it is obvious that a distinction must be drawn for purposes of any functional analysis. Then, too, the merchant might purchase or sell foreign exchange, or loans might be granted to various parties. A few isolated credit transactions would hardly justify the inclusion of such a merchant in the list of bankers. If, however, there were many transactions, and separate accounts were kept of these banking activities, we must recognize the emergence of a bank. In such enterprises the independence of the accounting unit is the more significant of the two criteria.

All early banks were banks of deposit, similar in essential functions to any modern bank of deposit, but, for two centuries at least, many features of banking business assumed special forms because these early banks made no use of cheques and found no negotiable commercial paper available as a means of placing their loans. They may be characterized as a primitive type of the bank of deposit. Almost every basic feature of their operation presents itself in a form unfamiliar to us, by reason of these important differences in the legal and administrative details of handling their credit. The whole credit structure was jeopardized by the absence of a satisfactory type of short-time paper. The banks were forced to engage directly in trade, and disastrous losses in Italy in the sixteenth century led to a demand for regulation which resulted in some undesirable curtailment of the credit activities of the banks.

II

Banks of deposit do not appear in mediæval Europe, even in their primitive form, until the close of the twelfth century or the beginning of the thirteenth.[3] Precise dates vary somewhat in different regions, and documentary material is so capriciously preserved that it is not wise to place much reliance upon any single piece of evidence. It was not a new form of economic activity, in any strict sense, because it is fairly clear that there were some deposit banks in Rome from the late years of the Republic. Banks were also to be found in the Near East both before and after the rise of Mohammed.[4] The legal basis of early banking was thus fully developed in Roman law of the period of the jurists, and these doctrines were not significantly modified until the concept of an implied contract appeared in the opinions on commercial law given by the Post glossators in the fourteenth century. The development of banking in the Middle Ages was, thus, a revival of an older institution rather than a new beginning. It is not impossible that some kind of contact may be established between banking in Imperial Rome and mediæval banking, but there is nothing in evidence now available to indicate any direct continuity in practice. Some have believed that the Jews played an active and important part in the maintenance of banking throughout the early Christian period, but recent studies indicate that the development of banking among the Jews began at a relatively late date.[5] It is not impossible that Syrian merchants coming to Europe from the Near East exercised some banking functions, but, on the whole, the presumption is against any specific continuity in the practice of deposit banking.

The legal principles upon which deposit banking was based never lost their validity, for the elementary principles were definitely embodied in all the shorter codes of Roman law that were drawn up during the

---

[3] Cf. Rota, Pietro, Storia delle banche, Milano, 1874. Aurelio Martin Alonso y Agustin Blasco Cirera, La banca a través de los tiempos, Barcelona, 1926. These useful general books are untrustworthy in many details, most especially in the critical period of the fourteenth, fifteenth, and sixteenth centuries. The chapters contributed by Pierre des Essars to the History of Banking in All Nations (Vol. III, New York, 1896) are unreliable.

[4] Westermann, W. L., "Warehousing and Trapezite Banking in Antiquity," Journal of Economic and Business History, Vol. III (1930), pp. 30–54. Herzog, Rudolph, Aus der Geschichte des Bankwesens im Altherthum, Geissen, 1919. Mitteis, L., "Trapezita," Zeitschrift der Savigny Stiftung, Vol. XIX, pp. 198–259. Platon, Georges, "Les banquiers dans le legislation de Justinien," Nouvelle Revue de Droit Français et Étranger, Vol. XXXIII (1909), pp. 5, 137, 289, 434. Preisigke, Friedrich, "Zur Buchführung der Banken," Archiv für Papyrusforschung, IV (1907), p. 95. Petra, G., "La tavolette cerate di Pompeii Rinvenuti ai 3 e 5 Juglio 1875," Atti della R. Accademia dei Lincei (Roma), 1875–76, Ser. 2, III, p. 155. Freundt, C., Wertpapiere im antiken und frühmittelalterlichen Rechte, Leipzig, 1910.

[5] Hoffman, Moses, Der Geldhandel der deutschen Juden während des mittelalters, Leipzig, 1910. Staats- und Sozialwissenschaftlichen Forschungen, G. Schmoller und Max Sering, No. 152. Schipper, Ignaz, "Anfänge des Kapitalismus bei den abendländischen Juden im frühen mittelalter," Zeitschrift für Volkswirtschaft, Sozialpolitik und Verwaltung, XV., pp. 501–64.

period of the migrations. The revival of the study of the full text of the Digest in the twelfth century was not a necessary prelude to the revival of banking. There was no period in which it would not have been lawful for a money-changer to accept a deposit of funds which he might employ in trade or lend to others, subject only to the obligation to repay the depositor on demand in coin of equivalent value. As there can be little doubt of the continuance of dealing in domestic and foreign coin, it is eminently possible that deposits were occasionally received, but this practice would not warrant the assumption that there was a sufficient volume of funds on deposit in current accounts to make credit creation possible.

There is a phase of credit development that immediately precedes the emergence of true banking. This stage is characterized by the occurrence of individual transactions in credit at such infrequent intervals that no significant development of clearance is possible. The general character of these activities appears clearly in the Low Countries in the late thirteenth century. In the last quarter of the century the Italian merchants were allowed by the authorities to establish "loan offices" *(tables de prêt)* in specified towns. The earliest dated grant is of 1280, but there is no reason to suppose that this grant for the town of Hulst was in fact the first. In the next two decades the institution was rapidly generalized.[6] In the larger towns more than one loan office might be authorized, but for the most part the privilege was held to confer some exclusive rights. Deposits were accepted, loans were made, and some of the funds were at times used in trade by the merchant-banker. Many, but not all, of the loans were pawnbrokers' loans on goods. Offices of this general type continued in this region until after 1450. In the course of this period some of them doubtless came to exercise banking functions, but the volume of their business at the close of the thirteenth century must be taken into consideration. There are documents giving records of the loans made at Tournai for the years 1260–1289, though the records for many years seem to be incomplete. For 1272 and 1273, however, the returns appear to be fully representative. There were 20 transactions in 1272 amounting in all to £1,384 11s. 6d. (Paris). The records for Nivelles in 1362 show 99 transactions, but the average for the years 1356 to 1388 is only 40.[7] Even if some allowance is made for omissions, it is evident that these loan offices did not regularly carry current accounts, and that the actual number of credit transactions was so small that these

---

[6] Bigwood, Georges, *Le régime juridique et économique du commerce de l'argent dans la Belgique du moyen age,* I., pp. 319–79. Académie Royale de Belgique, Classe des Lettres et des Sciences Morales et Politiques: Mémoires, IIe Série, XIV., Bruxelles, 1921.

[7] Bigwood, G., *op. cit.,* I., p. 368; II., pp. 103–261.

activities must be recognized as incidental and discontinuous. The earliest positive evidence of the holding of current accounts by these loan offices is for the years 1390, 1410, and 1418, when the office at Namur acted as fiscal agent for the town in collecting certain forced loans.[8] Even in this instance the banking activity seems to be distinctly less developed than it was in the Mediterranean countries at a much earlier date. But it is not necessary to attempt to fix any positive date for the development of the use of the current account in Belgium. For the moment, our chief concern is to show the importance of making a distinction between organized deposit banking and the mere making of loans and the acceptance of casual deposits.

In Latin and in the vulgar tongues, there are terms that must be literally translated as *money-changer* and *banker*. In some parts of Italy a real distinction ultimately develops between these terms, and we find in fact that the money-changer is indeed a dealer in domestic and foreign coin, whereas the banker holds deposits and lends credit. But these terms are by no means a safe guide in tracing the early history of banking. In Florence, in Catalonia, and in France the term *money-changer* was frequently, if not generally, applied to the private bankers. In parts of Italy, the terms *money-changer* and *banker* were used indiscriminately, at least as late as the fourteenth century.[9]

The references to bankers in the notarial documents of Genoa possess some special significance, however, because these documents throw light on various supplementary activities of these bankers. The printed extracts from the earliest of the notarial note-books, covering the years 1155 to 1164, contain references to thirteen bankers.[10] In some instances, the references appear only in the lists of witnesses to contracts, but in several instances the bankers are parties to contracts of partnership for trade. It would seem likely, therefore, that they were banker-merchants, accepting deposits which they utilized directly in trade. But even though it is evident that these bankers had extended their activities beyond dealings in domestic and foreign coin, there is no basis for an inference that they held current accounts on any appreciable scale. Unless we go beyond the documents, they must

---

[8] *Ibid.*, I., p. 434.

[9] La Sorsa, Saverio, *L'organizzazione dei cambiatori fiorentini nel medio evo,* p. 133, Cerignola, 1904, Statutes of 1299, art. 78. Lattes, Alessandro, *Il diritto commerciale nella legislazione statutaria delle citta italiane,* pp. 198–99, Milano, 1884, Cusumano, Vito, *Storia dei banchi delle Sicilia,* Roma, 1887, I., pp. 44 *ff.*, 71 *ff.*

[10] *Historiæ Patriæ Monumenta,* VI.; chartæ, II., Torino, 1853, 293–989. The names are: Albertson, Amicus, Baldo Baldus, Donaldeus, Gilbertus, Ingo Ingone, Hugo, Martinus, Museus, Nubelotus Nubeletus, Poncius, Raimundus, Sorleon. The references appear in the index under these names under the word Januensis.

thus be classed with the Belgian money-lenders, some of whom were likewise engaged in trade, and who were certainly accepting deposits. At Siena, there are references in 1156 to bankers who accept deposits, but without more details we cannot accept these references as evidence of the emergence of deposit banking.[11]

The financial activities of the Templars in England and in France disclose more explicitly the development of the current account in the later years of the twelfth century. Henry II. of England deposited funds with the Temple in 1182 and 1188 for use in the Crusade, and Philip Augustus deposited funds with the Templars and with the Knights of St. John. An account of 1202 shows that the Templars held the general receipts of the French Crown and were acting generally as the disbursing agency on royal account.[12] It seems evident that these activities continued, and that the scope of the banking business of the establishments of the Temple in France increased steadily. By 1250 accounts were held for Blanche of Castile and for various peers. The itemized records of some of these accounts which have survived show overdrafts, so that we must assume that the Templars were definitely financing the larger expenditures of the Crown and some of the Peers.[13] In the second half of the twelfth century the King of Aragon and several of the Catalan nobility were given loans by the Prior in Catalonia upon the security of stated revenues. There is no evidence that the Templars held current accounts for the King.[14] By 1212, the Templars at Paris were assisting in the collection and remittance of papal revenues. There is no specific evidence that these activities were continuously maintained thereafter, but the enlarged scope of financial activity on the part of the Temple is indicative of a development of new facilities.

For Italy, too, there is unmistakable evidence of the use of current accounts in the early years of the thirteenth century. We have two sheets from the ledger of a Florentine banker for the year 1211.[15] These sheets were used as guards in the binding of a codex of the Digest, and although they were somewhat damaged on some of the edges and badly worn in places, it has been possible to recover nearly the whole of the text. The entries are in Italian. They are one of the earliest

---

[11] Senigaglia, Q., *Le compagnie bancarie Senesi nei secoli XIII e XIV,* in Studi Senesi (1907–1908), Vols. XXIV, XXV; Vol. XXV, p. 24.

[12] Delisle, L., *Mémoire sur les operations financières des Templiers,* pp. 27, 40. Mémoires de l'Institut National de France, Académie des Inscriptions et Belles Lettres, XXXIII, IIe Partie, Paris, 1889.

[13] Delisle, L., *op. cit.,* pp. 32–33, 99.

[14] Miret y Sans, Joachim, *Les Cases de Templers y Hospitallers en Catalunya,* pp. 107–109, Barcelona, 1910.

[15] Santini, P., *Frammenti di un libro di banchieri fiorentini,* Giornali Storico della Letteratura Italiana, Vol. X (1887), pp. 161–96.

extant documents in the Florentine dialect, and the interest of the editor was primarily philological. The sheets were used on both sides, and the entries were made in two columns, but this division was merely a matter of convenience. Debtor and creditor items are not carefully separated. The amounts are not drawn off in the margins, nor are any balances given at the end of each account. The book thus represents the basic elements of the ledger, in as far as it is a statement of the accounts of particular individuals or partners with the banker. But it represents a transitional stage in the development of double entry bookkeeping, because the accounts are never presented in the form of an equation or balanced statement. There are references to other books, but only in such vague terms as "the old register" *(libro uekio)* or the "new memorandum" *(quaderno nuovo)*. It is difficult to identify the journal under either of these terms.

This prototype of the bank ledger shows conclusively, however, that the use of the current account was definitely established. The accounts cover parts of May and June, 1211. In some instances the entries relate to the last two weeks in June; a few items relate to transactions in May. Even with so small a fragment it is clear that there was much greater activity than in the loan offices in Belgium. The transactions, too, are specifically banking transactions: loans for a few months or for a year, on personal security; transfers of funds in bank; receipts and payments of specie. Some of the items are not dated, so that it is not possible to balance any of the accounts. It would seem, however, that some of them were definitely overdrawn.

III

The materials described above indicate clearly that banking functions were exercised by more than one kind of enterprise, even in the beginning. The Templars were active until the suppression of the order in 1312. Some of their activities in France were taken over by the Knights of St. John, but there is little to indicate that the order was an important factor in international finance in the fourteenth century. The great Italian trading companies became conspicuously important in the course of the thirteenth century, but early references to them are not very explicit in respect of their banking activities. It is significant, however, that loans made by Italians to German ecclesiastics were repaid at the Fairs of Champagne as early as 1213. By 1233, Sienese bankers were acting as fiscal agents for the Pope and a body of special privileges was rapidly built up. The bankers were authorized to lend to ecclesiastics such sums as might be necessary to meet the donations and grants customary at the time of induction into the various ecclesiastical offices and dignities.[16] Closely associated with this class of business was the general trade of northern France and Flanders centring in the Fair systems of Champagne and Flanders. The Italian companies played an important part in the business of these fairs, finance as well as general trade. Their services as agencies for the remittance of funds were deeply involved in the fair trade and seem to have furnished some means for the establishment of a primitive form of interregional clearance.[17]

The fairs also attracted a class of Italians and Jews who acted as money-changers and bankers. They constitute a special type, closely similar to the resident money-changers and bankers, but they possessed a number of special functions closely associated with the fairs. In the twelfth century, their activities were largely confined to dealings in domestic and foreign coin. Then two new functions appear. Descriptions of the fairs in the early thirteenth century show that many of the transactions were cleared by book transfers. When a merchant made purchases which he was not at the moment able to cover in specie, he took his creditor to a money-changer and promised payment through the money-changer at the close of the fair. It was assumed that the merchant would then be in funds through the sale of goods. In so far as payment through the bankers took the place of specie, some proportion of the total transactions were doubtless settled by clearance. This type of transaction was not uncommon in general commercial practice, but the effect was not the same. At the fairs there was no positive obligation to pay until the end of the fair. The promise to pay through the banker, thus, did not involve any loan on the part of the banker. The banker merely guaranteed payment. The effect was about equivalent to the endorsement of a modern promissory note.

This business, however, carried the bankers towards true credit activities. In some instances merchants found that their commitments for the close of the fair exceeded the receipts from the sale of goods. In this event they found themselves facing legal action for default, unless they could borrow funds to meet their immediate requirements. Loans repayable at the next fair appear in the records at the Champagne fairs as early as 1218, though the practice was not definitely established until the close of the century. The loan for the interval

---

[16] Schulte, Aloys, *Geschichte des mittelalterlichen Handels und Verkehrs zwischen Westdeutschland und Italien mit Ausschluss von Venedig*, Leipzig, 1900, I, 231–35. Senigaglia, *op. cit.*, Studi Senesi, XXIV, pp. 163–64.

[17] Bourquelot, F., *Études sur les foires de Champagne et de Brie*, II., 103. Mémoires de l'Académie des Inscriptions et de Belles Lettres, Paris, 1865. The use of the fairs as a term of payment can be traced continuously from 1159. The loans and remittances of the great trading houses were built up on this practice in the course of the following century.

between fairs became a characteristic feature of commercial life that persisted in some centres, such as Lyons, until late in the eighteenth century. This highly important type of short-time loan constituted the chief form of loan on the part of fair bankers. In the early period it was based on the letter of the fair, or perhaps even on a book entry. In the fifteenth and sixteenth centuries such loans were made on bills of exchange, drawn in favour of the lender.[18]

Finally, there were the sedentary money-changers and bankers who had an office only in one town. In some localities this type of banker appears as early as any of the others, but they became more important in the fourteenth and fifteenth centuries. After the failures of the great Italian trading companies in the fourteenth century, the sedentary bankers became the dominant factor in banking in Italy, Spain, and France. Conditions in Central Europe were different. The rise of the great Austrian banking houses in the fifteenth century certainly reduced the small local bankers to a distinctly secondary rôle, but we do not hear enough about them to give us any precise notion of their significance in that region. Offices for dealings in domestic and foreign coin were established at Augsburg, Lübeck, Hamburg, Aachen, Dortmund, Erfurt, Nürnberg, Frankfort-am-M., and Strassburg.[19] One would infer, therefore, that private money-changers were not very active. As in other regions, the functions of these offices were extended by the acceptance of deposits and, in some instances, deposit banks may have developed.

---

[18] Bourquelot, F., *op. cit.*, II., 118–46. Huvelin, P., *Essai historique sur le droit des marchés et des foires*, pp. 544–69, Paris, 1897.

[19] Lattes, A., *op. cit.*, pp. 217–19; Cusumano, V., *op. cit., passim*. Lattes E., *op. cit.*

References in Spanish ordinances apply primarily to sedentary bankers and money–changers: A. Diaz de Montalvo, *Ordenanzas reales de Castilla*, Lib. V., Tit. VIII., L. 1 (1445, 1455), in *Codigos Españoles*, VI., p. 410. *Novissima, Recopilacion*, Lib. IX., Tit. III., L. 1 (1435, 1436, 1455); *loc. cit.*, L. 2 (25 Julio, 1499). *Codigos Españoles*, IX., p. 183; *ibid.*, Lib. XI., Tit. XXXII., L. 1 (1548); *loc. cit.*, L. 7 (18 Julio, 1590). Cristobal Espejo y Julian Paz, *Las antiguas ferias de Medina del Campo*, pp. 71–128, Valladolid, 1912.

For France, see Vigue, Marcel, *La banque à Lyon*, pp. 50–52, Paris, 1903. Paris, Archives Nationales, KK, 5, *Livre des changeurs du Trésor*, 1335–43; KK, 15, *Livre des changeurs du Trésor*, 1397–1405, Z 1b, 286–90, *Registres des changeurs du Royaume*, 1456–1601; AD, XI., 1, *Agents de change et banquiers*, 1572–1789. These materials were hurriedly examined in 1927 and 1929. They indicate roughly the general character of the development of private banking in France, but without the letters and accounts of banking firms the study could not be carried very far.

For Germany, Ehrenberg, R., *Das Zeitalter der Fugger*, Jena, 1896 (1922), I., pp. 85–90, 186–197. See also the later literature on the Fuggers by Max Jansen, Jacob Strieder, and A. Schulte. Kulischer, J., "Warenhandler und Geld-ausleiher im Mittelalter," *Zeitschrift für Volkswirtschaft, Sozialpolitik und Verwaltung*, XVII (1908), pp. 202–4, 217–19. Marperger, Paul Jacob, *Beschreibung der Banken*, Wien 1717.

Public banks of deposit were established at Barcelona in 1401, and at Valencia in 1407. These institutions did not displace the private banks, but as they served as fiscal agents for the towns and provinces they restricted in some measure the scope of the activities of the private bankers. Some writers have classified these public banks as "giro" banks, assuming them to be similar in function to the banks established at Venice in 1584, 1587, and 1619, and to the Bank of Amsterdam of 1609. The banks at Barcelona and Valencia were, however, true banks of deposit, identical in all their general features with the private banks of deposit in Catalonia,[20] Spain, Italy, and France. As they were administered conservatively they exhibit the primary features of the primitive bank of deposit even more clearly than the private banks. At Barcelona, the Bank of Deposit retained its original form until 1609, though both the private and public banks in Italy introduced new features in the sixteenth century, which created some circulating credit. The Bank of Saint George at Genoa exercised banking functions during the years 1407 to 1445, and again after 1586, but these activities of the Bank have not been extensively studied, despite the abundance of material.[21]

Deposit banking developed rapidly in all the more important commercial centres of Europe in the course of the thirteenth century. The wide extent of this development was, undoubtedly, fostered by the influence of the Templars and the Italian merchants following the fairs. The relative uniformity of practice was also fostered at this time, and later by the influence of Roman Law upon the commercial law. Although the amount of material varies considerably in different regions, there is no reason to doubt the actual existence of important banking activities throughout the greater part of Europe. The dearth of material in France for the fourteenth and fifteenth centuries is especially unfortunate.

The early history of banking is in all regions dominated by a highly characteristic form of deposit bank, which differs in a number of particulars from the practice of the modern bank of deposit as well as from the modern bank of deposit and issue. Full analysis of the functions of the primitive bank of deposit requires more material than is available in many of the localities where we know banking was carried on, but a general description of the primitive bank of deposit can be given if careful use is made of the large masses of material available in Florence, Venice, Sicily, Naples, and Barcelona.

---

[20] Usher, Abbott Payson, "Deposit Banking in Barcelona," *Journal of Economic and Business History* (1931), IV., pp. 121–55.

[21] Sieveking, H., *Genueser Finanzwesen vom 12 bis 14 Jahrhundert*, pp. 1–75, Freiburg, 1898. II. Volkswirtschaftliche Abhandlungen der Badischen Hochschule, I., 3e Heft. Marengo, E., Manfroni, C., and Pessango, G., *Il banco in San Giorgio*, pp. 193–217, Genova, 1911.

Important material is available in some other places, notably at Genoa and Valencia, and the resources of Florence, Venice, and Barcelona have not been exhausted, but material now at hand is sufficient to establish the primary features of the primitive bank of deposit. Local variations from the general type are not of great significance for the fourteenth and fifteenth centuries.

IV

The distinctive features of the primitive bank of deposit were largely derived from the predominant use of the verbal contract.[22] Written contracts were valid, but until the sixteenth century the use of the written contract was restricted and it was regarded as a means of dealing with a number of situations that could not readily be provided for by the usual verbal contracts. In order to facilitate the establishment of the content and authenticity of contracts, the notarial system of Rome was developed and extended. The verbal contracts of mediæval commerce were thus made before a notary and witnesses. The transaction was recorded in the register of the notary and became a matter of public record. The record was accepted as competent evidence of the content of the contract, unless it could be shown that the record was incorrect. The most effective defence against the record was the establishment of an alibi. If the party alleged to have made the contract could prove that he was not in town on the day stated, the record would be overthrown, because the contract required the presence of both parties to make the formal statement of the contract and to accept the contract.[23] Great pains were taken to make the notarial registers absolutely trustworthy, but, like the records of our modern registries of deeds, they were merely evidences of the actual contract.

---

[22] The critical establishment of the views presented rests primarily upon the interpretation of a number of technical terms. Some of these terms acquire new meanings in the sixteenth and seventeenth centuries, others have misleading connotations to the modern student. The wide differences of opinion about early banks have been due to the different readings given these terms. The present study is based upon a glossary of Catalan terms constructed upon rigidly historical principles. The interpretation of each term has been determined by dated passages in which the context affords an absolutely unambiguous clue to the meaning. The more difficult terms have been discussed with Prof. J. M. D. Ford, and with Jacme Llorens, a native Catalan, now studying economics at Harvard. The interpretation of Italian terms is based upon the glossary of mediæval Italian business terms which is being prepared by Miss Florence Edler for the Mediæval Academy of America. Problems of translation are merely incidental, for the terms used in the documents themselves must needs be rendered into modern Spanish, Catalan, or Italian.

[23] Freundt, C., *Wertpapiere,* I, p. 69. Justinian, *Institutes,* III, xix, 12.

The Journals of the early banks were given the legal status of a notarial register. Private bankers were required to swear that their Journals were a faithful record of all the transactions of the bank.[24] At Barcelona, the Journals of the Bank of Deposit were kept by notaries and thus were merely a special notarial record. The entries in the Journal were required to be made without intervening blank spaces, no erasures or cancellations might be made unless duly described in the margin, and no leaves might be torn out. These rules have left traces in modern commercial law, but the background has changed. In the Middle Ages, the Journal contained the only legally valid written record of most of the contracts between the bank and its customers. It was much more than an account book, and for this reason it was considered essential that the Journal entry should contain a full statement of the details of the transaction. The private bankers were at times lax, and in Italy there was a strong disposition to reduce the entry to the simplest possible form, but the basic facts must needs be stated. The Journal entry of a bank differed from the ordinary notarial record in the omission of all record of witnesses. The Florentine ledger of 1211, however, preserved a record of witnesses for certain types of transactions. This is the most impressive single indication of the extremely primitive character of that bank register. Because the Journal was a legal record in which cancellations could not lightly be made, it was not a book of original entry. In the Bank of Deposit at Barcelona, the account in the Ledger was ordinarily checked if any funds were to be transferred, or if any loan were to be made. If a private bank were large enough to have separate bookkeepers for the two books, the Journal entry would be made only after an appropriate memorandum had been received from the keeper of the Ledger.

These legal attributes of the Journal tended to simplify the details of paper work at the bank. It was not necessary to require separate promissory notes from customers who were granted a loan, because the Journal entry was itself competent legal evidence of the contract. It was not necessary to provide the customer with a pass-book or with any certificate of deposit, because the Journal was a public register of contracts that was open to the inspection of the customer. It soon came to be regarded as a breach of confidence to allow other persons to inspect the account of a customer of the bank, but in the early period it is fairly certain that the information in the Journal could not be kept confidential.

---

[24] Lattes, A., *op. cit.*, p. 205. Covers specifically Genoa, Piacenza, Milan, Bologna, and Venice. Cusumano, V., *op. cit.*, I, p. 131. *Constitutions y altres drets de Cathalunya, compilats en virtud del cap de las corts . . . celebrados en la vila de Montso*, 1585 (Barcelona, 1587. Hereafter cited, *Constitutions de Cathalunya*). James II at the Cortes at Barcelona, 1299, ch. vi, p. 384.

All bankers kept a ledger or some book that was a prototype of the ledger. The fragments of the accounts of the Templars at Paris and some of the records of Père des Caus and Andreu d'Olivella in Barcelona suggest that the early bankers were likely to keep a large number of separate records. The defect of their bookkeeping consisted in having too many records of particular accounts and no general analysis of the business as a whole. There is not enough material now extant to make it possible to establish the details of development during the thirteenth and fourteenth centuries. Cash accounts or separate accounts of receipts and expenditures appeared at an early date.[25] Balances and analyses of the enterprise as a whole, if made at all, were commonly separate documents and few have survived. There were considerable differences in the practices of the various regions in all these respects. At Barcelona, there is no evidence that there was any general analysis of the affairs of the bank, until late in the sixteenth or early seventeenth century. Italian practice may have been better, but the descriptions in the texts afford no basis for any positive statement. The officials of the Bank of Deposit at Barcelona were obliged to balance the accounts every two years, when new Administrators took office, but the extant record of such an audit for the year 1433 shows that it was no more than a general check on the accuracy of the arithmetic.[26] We have all the elements from which a balance sheet can be constructed, but the officers did not themselves draw up any comprehensive statement of the affairs. The private bankers may have made some audit when they started a new ledger, but there is abundant ground for doubt. For the most part, they merely copied off the individual balances of the open accounts. It is hardly surprising that there were many failures. The average banker had no exact summary statement of his commitments. We must assume that banking policy consisted chiefly in keeping some actual cash in hand, extending loans to promising customers, and making some investments in trade.

Deposits fell into two classes: general deposits and conditioned

---

[25] Barcelona, Archivo del Real Patrimonio (hereafter ARP), 2380. Libre de Père des Caus e d'en Andreu d'Olivella . . . datas e rebudes. Cusumano, V., *op. cit.*, I., 129. Bensa, E., *Francesco di Marco da Prato*, pp. 194–208, 448–66, Milano, 1928. Marengo Manfroni, Pessango, *op. cit.*, p. 198.

[26] Archivo Historico Municipal de Barcelona (hereafter AMB), Llevament fet per en Marti Gariera, 1433. There is no formal provision in the ordinances for any audit of the books of the Bank of Deposit earlier than 1513, but examinations of the bank were made twice each year after 1476. AMB, Reg. d'Ordinacions, 1510–18, f. 67v; *ibid.*, 1471–79, f. 111.

The fragments of accounts studied by Cusumano are largely of the sixteenth century. The accounts of private banks available at Genoa have not been studied with reference to these aspects of accounting, though the brief notes of Marengo, Manfroni, and Pesango imply that there was some general analysis at an early date.

deposits. The general deposits were demand obligations on current account comparable in all respects to the deposit in a modern bank. The depositors fell into three general classes: individuals and corporations owning real property, or holders of funded debts; public bodies who carried current accounts covering all, or at least a part, of their general receipts and expenses; lastly, the business men and merchants. The deposit accounts of these early banks thus exhibit the diversities of expenditure and interest characteristic of the modern community. Public authorities and merchants carried active accounts, and were usually applicants for loans. The holders of the less active accounts were the landed gentry, widows, orphans, and ecclesiastical corporations. Their revenues were paid into the banks and drawn down gradually for personal expenditure. This group was the great resource of the state for loans, though the mercantile community must not be excluded. Long-time loans were common throughout Europe on the basis of the sale of a rent. The legal concept was readily assimilated to feudal law, and because it was in essence a sale of property there could be no infraction of the usury laws. As these rent charges could be redeemed at pleasure in most jurisdictions after the early thirteenth century, they were, in effect, mortgage bonds without a fixed date for redemption. These instruments present special features in many regions, wherever the revenues were collected directly by the mortgagee. In Spain and in France the rent charges were scarcely distinguishable from a modern mortgage bond. A fixed income was paid the mortgagee during the life of the bond. The property remained under the control of the owner, and in the case of pledges on revenues of state the state collected its revenues at its discretion.

In Barcelona, all borrowing by the city or province took the form of the sale of incomes guaranteed by pledges of specific revenues. Non-negotiable documents were issued, and in nearly all instances, after 1401, the Bank of Deposit acted as the fiscal agent of the city in selling or redeeming these securities, and paying the semi-annual interest charges. At Genoa, the loans were handled in a somewhat more primitive fashion, as the syndicates who lent the money assumed direct charge of the collection of revenue. Venetian practice was varied. Forced loans were levied on many occasions in the fifteenth and sixteenth centuries. At times, banking privileges were associated with these loans.[27]

Conditional deposits were a characteristic feature of the primitive bank of deposit. In their simplest form they consisted of actual

---

[27] Sieveking, H., *Genueser Finanzwesen mit besonderer Berücksichtigung der Casa San Giorgio,* Freiburg, 1898. *I prestiti della Repubblica di Venezia,* Padova, 1929. (R. Accademia dei Lincei, Documenti Finanziari della Repubblica di Venezia, Ser. III., Vol. I., Parte I.) Lattes, E., *op. cit.,* pp. 41–44.

deposits of specie to be paid to a designated party at a fixed date or after the performance of some definite act.[28] Funds to be paid on the transfer of property, sums to be paid over on dowries or marriage settlements, sums due in settlement of judgments in the courts, the price of merchandise to be delivered at a later date, might all give rise to conditioned deposits. The payor placed the funds in the hands of the banker with an explicit understanding that they would be transferred to the payee when the conditions of their agreement had been fulfilled. Such funds did not constitute a part of the ordinary current account of either party. The payor was obviously barred from diverting such funds to other uses, and the payee could not use them because they did not become his property until the final transfer was made. In their primitive form conditioned deposits did not lead to any use of credit, but small changes made them useful in an important type of credit transaction. The banker might allow a customer to overdraw his demand account in the ledger on the security afforded by a credit due from a third party in the record of conditioned deposits, or against an engagement of the borrower to repay the banker at a stated time. This operation would have the same effect as the discounting of a negotiable bill of exchange or promissory note, although different in form. There is evidence of such transactions in the audit of the books of the Bank of Deposit at Barcelona in 1433, and in the Journals of Père des Caus and Andreu d'Olivella. Such transactions continued to be a significant feature of banking until the doctrine of negotiability was fully established and simpler means of effecting the same end were available.[29]

The loans made by these early bankers commonly resembled the modern overdraft. The loan was created by transfers or withdrawals from the ledger account in excess of the credit. When the entries were in the ledger, we have no means of knowing what charges were imposed, but it is evident that no interest would be paid on any sums not actually used. The transaction differed from the modern overdraft by cheque, because each operation must needs have the consent of the banker.[30] Transfers from the current account of the primitive

---

[28] ARP, 2375. Manual de Père des Caus e Andreu d'Olivella, ff. 1–30v, *passim*. AMB, Libre Major de la Taula de Cambi, 1403–4. AMB, Reg. d'Ordinacions, 1519–30, October 27, 1527, f. 175. AMB, Llevament . . . 1433, ff. 31–48v, 53v. Cusumano, V., *op. cit.*, I., 163. Lattes, E., *op. cit.*, ordinance of 1421, pp. 47–48. Lattes, A., *op. cit.*, 224, n. 53, covers Novara, Milan, Como, Genoa, Piacenza, Florence, and Ferrara.

[29] AMB, Manual de la Taula, 1602. Balans del llibre de deposits, 1611–12. See also material cited by A. Lattes; the statutes of the Italian towns remained in force, and in some instances the revisions of the statutes are of the sixteenth century.

[30] This discussion of the overdraft rests mainly upon study of the early Ledgers of the Bank of Deposit and the Llevament . . . of 1433. There are so many references to the ordinances that it is evident that the references cited

bank could regularly be made only in the presence of both parties, and, consequently, the client could not overdraw without the knowledge and consent of the banker, or the connivance of a clerk. The record in the Journal had sufficient legal status to make a formal promissory note superfluous, and the use of supplementary documents was confined to special cases involving the Crown, or loans to the City or Province.

The non-negotiable bill of exchange, which came into extensive use in the second half of the fourteenth century, was an important factor in the credit business of banks. A bill could not be discounted in the modern fashion, but exchange could be bought and sold. The essential objects of the modern transaction could be accomplished in various ways, though it is impossible to trace all these operations specifically in the accounts. We know, positively, that the proceeds of many loans made to the Crown by P. des Caus and A. d'Olivella were given the King in the form of bills of exchange on Sicily. We know, too, that exchange could be purchased with bank credit. Bills might also serve, indirectly, as a basis for a loan. The characteristic transaction at the fairs was the loan of present purchasing power against a bill payable to the lender at a designated fair, either in the same town or elsewhere. A merchant could not, however, raise money directly on an accepted bill, but a banker could permit the merchant to overdraw his current account, with or without a supplementary engagement as to the details of repayment. Bills play a large part in mediæval and early modern credit operations, because at an early date the interest charges were admitted to be outside the prohibitions of canon law. The purchase and sale of currency of a different jurisdiction required no explicit recognition of interest as such, and most early bills merely state the amount of money given and the sum to be paid. In some regions, the rate of interest was openly stated, and inter-fair loans were definitely legitimated by civil statutes at an early date.

Although the bankers had several important avenues for commercial

---

below for 1435 and 1437 are characteristic of a continuous practice. AMB, Clavaria de la Ciutat . . . 1472, Oath of 1435, f. 5v; Reg. de Deliberacions, 1433–37, November 19, 1437, f. 192. The Journals of P. des Caus and Andreu d'Olivella imply that their loans to the Crown were secured by formal notes and assignments of specific revenues, so that they were not overdrafts in the sense of a loan unsecured by any supplementary document. We can thus draw no inferences from the mere fact that there were debit balances in the accounts of the King of France and various French nobles with the Templars. Cusumano pays no attention to this problem in his study of the Sicilian material, though there must be conclusive evidence in the fragments of ledgers available. The Venetian ordinance of June 2, 1524, describes the practice explicitly (Lattes, E., op. cit., p. 87), and Contarini (1584) clearly regards the practice as the most characteristic mode of lending (Lattes, E., op. cit., p. 125). Although the evidence outside of Barcelona is less adequate than one would desire, the deficiency is due primarily to the inattention of the text writers and to the neglect of even the bank ledgers that survive. In this respect the Italian sources have been very inadequately utilized.

loans, they were closely associated with trade throughout the period.[31] In some instances, the mercantile interests were more important than their banking interests, and in nearly all regions bankers commonly had considerable sums invested in trade. These investments were the greatest single source of weakness to the banking houses of the early period.

The absence of cheques made inter-bank relations somewhat complex, but some contacts existed from an early date. Bankers kept accounts with each other. They could thus make some use of each other's facilities, though the authorities always distrusted such relationships.[32] In some instances, it amounted to an evasion of the banker's liability to meet the requirements of depositors on demand. It was not quite right to take the client around to other bankers to get the money. The Bank of Deposit at Barcelona feared lest the private bankers should deliberately attempt to use the reserves of the Bank of Deposit as a means of expanding their own activities. There were thus repeated prohibitions of the acceptance of the accounts of private bankers at the Bank of Deposit.

V

Commercial law exhibits a positive bias in favour of verbal contracts all through the fifteenth century, but exceptions were made. Some transactions in the banks were accompanied by written documents, and in some instances the written document soon became the controlling element in the transaction. The modern cheque grows out of this gradual development in the use of written orders drawn against current accounts. It is important to distinguish between the recognition of written orders in special cases and the frank acceptance of the cheque as a general means of effecting transfer or payments. The transition from a limited use of cheques to their general recognition occupied nearly a century and a half.

An exception to the rule, requiring the personal presence of the

---

[31] AMB, Caja: documentos notariales y lettres de cambion, *passim*. AMB, unclassified sheets; articles of partnership for a bank, March 15, 1460. AMB, Reg. d'Ordinacions, 1433–45, fol. 63. Lattes, A., *op. cit.*, p. 208. Cusumano, *op. cit.*, I., pp. 137, 143–48.

[32] This direct use of accounts in other banks is frequently described by modern writers as if cheques were drawn. The Barcelona material is most explicit. ARP, 2375, Manual de P. des Caus e A. d'Olivella, *passim*. AMB, Libre Major de la Taula, 1403–4, *passim*. At Venice, in 1527, even when some use was being made of cheques, the ordinance reads, "when a person comes to demand his money, the bankers often take him to another bank and transfer credit to him in that bank." Lattes, E., *op. cit.*, p. 91.

client, was frequently made by recognizing servants or messengers as agents of the client. Such a practice was not inconsistent with the concepts associated with the system of verbal contracts. Agency was recognized at an early date, and, although a formal power of attorney was required for many kinds of transactions, much business could be done by agents whose quality rested upon less rigorous proof. The Journals of Père des Caus and Andreu d'Olivella of Barcelona disclose withdrawals by servants or messengers in four instances in the period between July 20 and August 4, 1377. The sums involved were respectively: £60 10s. 0d.; £3 6s. 0d.; £72 0s. 0d.; £36 0s. 0d. In the same interval deposits were received by messenger in three instances; for sums as follows: £165 0s. 0d.; £643 10s. 0d.; £400 0s. 0d.[33] It is unfortunate that we have none of the papers that must have been used in such cases, as it would be interesting to know to what degree they possessed the external features of the modern cheque. It must be evident, however, that we cannot classify as a cheque an order which merely gave the bearer authority to act as agent for the client.

This problem of the legal significance of a written order or assignment is conspicuously involved in the documents printed by Bensa from the Datini archives at Prato. The papers of Francesco di Marco, an international merchant and banker of the late fourteenth century, include a considerable number of assignments on the current accounts held by the banker. In their general form, they present an extraordinary resemblance to the modern cheque, and Bensa has not hesitated to classify them as cheques. It must be recognized, however, that these documents precede by a wide interval any general use of a cheque by *private* persons. It is difficult to accept them as cheques when there is so large a body of material that indicates serious resistance to the acceptance of the concept in any form and especial resistance to any general use of such a device by private persons.[34] These documents, however, are not without special features that might easily justify their use as exceptions to the general rules in favour of verbal contracts. Three of the documents published were drawn upon the banking office by a client not at that time in town.[35] An instrument of this general character might well have been recognized as a kind of bill of exchange. The general features of the instrument correspond closely with the contemporary bills. The banking house did a considerable business with bills and might well have been willing to recognize an instrument of this general character. The other

---

[33] ARP, 2375. Manual de P. des Caus e A. d'Olivella, ff. 16, 18, 22, 23v, 26, 27v, 28v, 30v.

[34] Bensa, E., *op. cit.*, pp. 164–66, 352–58.

[35] *Ibid.*, p. 352. See also, Bigwood, G., *op. cit.*, I., pp. 648–49; II., p. 316 an isolated text of 1306.

78919

documents, drawn in favour of a party in town by a client in town, present a problem which cannot be solved without more material. In all probability these documents possessed no certain status in court. They imply a relationship that extended beyond mere agency, but we have no evidence that any court would have recognized these implications. These documents were thus prototypes of the modern cheque, rather than true cheques.

The private bankers at Venice, at the beginning of the fifteenth century, permitted non-residents to use cheques. "It has been the custom of the banks of deposit," runs the ordinance of 1421, "to make transfers for non-residents up to the amount of their deposits on the presentation of written orders, because they can only use their funds in the form of credits in the bank. . . ."[36] The privilege led to some abuses. Credits in the banks were being bought and sold at a discount, as compared with specie. Such purchases and sales were prohibited, and the prohibition was reiterated subsequently. Without some study of bank journals it is impossible to be certain of the nature of these transactions. It is clear, however, that the practices arose out of concessions made to non-residents, and the basic privilege seems to have continued in force.

Among residents, written instruments first came into use in the transaction of official business, but the practices of the public officials require some distinctions to be made. In some instances, the written instruments were merely orders and memoranda for accounting purposes. Even though they were required, they were not the legal authority for the payment made by the bank. In 1435, the Administrators of the Bank of Deposit were forbidden to transfer any funds on order of the City Treasurer unless he presented "a warrant from the Councillors addressed to the Administrators of the Bank and sealed with the seal of the City. In this warrant . . . there shall be given the name of the party in whose favour the Treasurer wishes to transfer funds, and the amount to be assigned and recorded in the books, in order that the Administrators may be required to file these warrants and that they may be produced when their accounts are examined."[37]

---

[36] Lattes, E., *op. cit.*, p. 47. The interpretation given by E. Lattes cannot be sustained if the critical terms are read with the meanings established by other documents of the period. Important discussions of this ordinance are furnished by Allessandro Latte, *op. cit.*, p. 233, and by F. Ferrara, "Gli antichi banchi di Venezia," in *Nuova Antologia di Scienze,* Lettere ed Arte, XVI., p. 453. The translation given above follows these commentaries. Unfortunately the commentary accompanying the text has been uncritically copied, and some writers declare without qualification that the Venetian banks issued demand notes. This ordinance is the only passage upon which such a statement could be based. *Cf.* C. F. Dunbar, "The Bank of Venice," *Quarterly Journal of Economics,* VI., p. 316.

[37] AMB, Clavaria, f. 7.

It must be noted that the accounts of the City stood in the name of the Treasurer, so that his verbal order was no less necessary than this accompanying document. Such a document must thus be classified as an accounting memorandum, although it was in form an order on the Bank, which, without this text description, might erroneously be identified with a cheque.[38]

The accounts of the Province of Catalonia in the Bank of Deposit presented a different problem. When these deposits were first authorized in 1413, it was stipulated that no payments might be made from the account except upon presentation of a warrant signed by all three of the deputies who had charge of the affairs of the Province.[39] In such a case, we must regard the written order as the primary authority for the transfer. The account stood in the names of the three deputies. The order signed by all three was the only valid authority for transfer of funds. The person presenting the order was merely a messenger or agent of the Committee of three deputies. Later, when unanimous consent was no longer required, the Bank was allowed to recognize a warrant signed by a single deputy, if the payment had been duly voted by the commission.[40]

The City of Palermo, likewise, used written orders in handling City funds, from an early date in the fifteenth century. These orders were signed by the Prætor, the chief executive officer, or by one or more of the three deputies who assisted him.[41] Cusumano assumes that these documents had the status of cheques. Royal officials in various regions also used written documents, but no bank assignments are available for the fifteenth century.

The Sicilian documents of the late fifteenth century contain a formula which Cusumano assumes to refer to the cheque (polissa), but we have no clear references to the use of cheques until the early sixteenth century. There is evidence of general use of cheques prior to 1530, in Sicily, in Barcelona, and in Venice, and a strong presumption in favour of early use in Naples. In Sicily and Naples the practice developed continuously without interference from the authorities. In Venice, the use of cheques was absolutely prohibited, November 6, 1526. In Barcelona, the Bank of Deposit was allowed to recognize only the cheques drawn by the City Councillors, but the private bankers were allowed to recognize them.[42] The text of the ordinance in Barce-

---

[38] Even in 1553 the Treasurer was required to transact business in person at the bank. AMB, Reg. d'Ordinacions, 1549–59, fol. 101.

[39] Llibre dels Quatre Senyals del General de Cathalunya, Barcelona, 1634. Cort del any, 1413, ch. 12, p. 22.

[40] AMB, Reg. de Del., 1596, f. 19, January 8, 1596.

[41] Cusumano, V., op. cit., I., pp. 273–76. The earliest text cited is of 1443.

[42] Cusumano, V., op. cit., I., pp. 233, 280–89. Lattes, E., op. cit., p. 91. Ajello P., I depositi, la fade di credito e le polizi dei banchi di Napoli, in Filan-

lona states explicitly the objection to general acceptance of the cheque. "Inasmuch as experience has shown that there have been in the past many abuses by reason of the fact that many parties able to come in person to the said bank make transfers and entries in the bank by orders signed with their name directed to the keeper of the Journal which seems to lead to the discredit of the said bank: Therefore the Honourable Councillors and Syndics establish and ordain that henceforth the keeper of the Journal of the Bank of Deposit shall not be allowed to record any transfer by reason of any cheque or warrant drawn by any individual, unless such person . . . be present in person at the bank or be represented by his lawful attorney; excepting only in the case of some Councillor of the City, during the year of his Councillorship, who, by reason of the dignity of his office, ought not and is not permitted to come like other individuals to the bank."[43] Although provision was made for a bank messenger to take statements of transfers at the homes of the clients of the bank, there were attempts to make use of cheques at the Bank of Deposit. Depositors, at times, gave a power of attorney to the keeper of the Journal or to some other officer of the Bank, but the authorities prohibited these practices in 1567. Finally, in 1609, a new public bank was established, which was authorized to accept cheques.[44]

VI

Banks of deposit retained some of their primitive characteristics, even after the cheque came into use, for some of the special features of their operations were due to the lack of negotiable paper. The investments of the bank were necessarily different in character from what they are to-day, and the details of many credit operations were affected. The development of the doctrine of negotiability was thus of critical importance to the history of banking. The emergence of true negotiable paper transformed deposit banking and made possible the bank of issue. Most of the present confusion in the treatment of the early history of banking is due to the failure of many writers to recognize

---

gieri (1882), VII., pp. 646–47. AMB, Reg. d'Ordinacions, 1519–30, f. 179*v*, October 29, 1527. AMB, Reg. de Deliberacions 1530, ff. 26*v*–27, July 11, 1530.

[43] AMB, Reg. d'Ordinacions, 1519–30, ff. 179*v*–180, October 29, 1527. Many written documents were, however, received from the Treasurer of the City, the Treasurer of Majorca, the Deputies of the province, and from attorneys. On various special days the bookkeepers were required to enter these transactions outside of banking hours. *Ibid.*, f. 176*v*.

[44] AMB, Reg. d'Ordinacions, 1519–30, f. 177, October 29, 1527. AMB, Ordinacions de la Taula, 1567, f. 3. AMB, Reg. d'Ordinacions, 1608–15, f. 38*v*, October 10, 1609.

the intimate relationship between the history of banking and the history of commercial paper. Although extensive use had been made of "order" clauses and "bearer" clauses in the remittance contracts of the Middle Ages, these clauses merely set up an agency which differed in vital respects from the full transfer of rights embodied in a mature concept of negotiability. In external form these early documents seem to resemble our modern commercial paper, but in actual legal properties they were profoundly different. They constitute only a preliminary step towards modern commercial paper.[45]

Upon the general introduction of the written contract in the thirteenth and fourteenth centuries a bill of exchange emerged which presented none of the superficial elements of resemblance to modern paper. This was due to the explicit inclusion in the new instrument of all the four parties involved. The typical bill of the fifteenth century designated by name: (1) the party addressed—the payor; (2) the party who would present the bill for payment—the presentor or payee; (3) the party who had given consideration for the bill—the remittor; and, lastly (4), the maker of the bill. In the earlier remittance contracts the presentor was not named. The maker contracted to pay the stated amount to the remittor, or his duly constituted agent. The "order" clause was the most general form used to cover this appointment of an agent to receive the funds, but, despite its suggestiveness to the modern mind, this clause was never more than an authorization for one formal appointment of a specific presentor or recipient of the funds. The inclusion of this presentor in the mercantile bill of the fourteenth and fifteenth centuries made the order clause unnecessary. For many kinds of transactions, too, it was not necessary to arrange in advance for the appointment of an agent.

The position of the presentor at this time differed from that of the modern endorsee in three respects: his agency was automatically extinguished by the death of his principal, the remittor; his agency might be revoked; and, if legal proceedings were necessary, suit must needs be brought in the name of the principal. For promissory notes, rather than for bills of exchange, considerable use was made of a "bearer" clause. Possession of the instrument was sometimes interpreted as sufficient evidence of appointment as agent of the principal,

---

[45] The present account is based on the later German writing: Freundt, C., *Das Wechselrecht der Post glossatoren,* 2 vols., Leipzig, 1899, 1909. Schaps, Georg, *Zur Geschichte des Wechselindossaments,* Stuttgart, 1892. Hecht, Felix, *Ein Beitrag zur Geschichte der Inhaberpapiere in der Niederlanden,* Erlangen, 1869. These works supplant the older German writing to such an extent that references to the extensive earlier literature would serve no useful purpose. A fairly adequate account of these matters is furnished by Holdsworth, W. S., *A History of English Law,* VIII., pp. 113–70, London, 1922–26.

but the lawyers became more rigid in their doctrine and came to insist upon independent proof of an appointment as agent. The "bearer" clause thus became less useful in the course of the fourteenth and fifteenth centuries. The development of the doctrine of negotiability brought about important changes in the legal relationships among the parties to these commercial contracts. Without extensive changes in the forms of these documents there was an important transformation in their legal attributes, which made possible extensive revisions and developments of commercial practice.

There is no explicit evidence of any real break with older practices and doctrines until the second quarter of the sixteenth century, and it is equally clear that the new legal doctrines were not fully established in any country earlier than 1650. But only in 1700 can we assume that the primary types of commercial paper are fully negotiable. A critical period in the history of banking is thus complicated by this slow transition from non-negotiable to negotiable paper. If we are to avoid serious errors in the interpretation of banking practice, it is essential to have some appreciation of the timing of this process of development.

The change in the law followed changes in business practice, so that we must look to the activities of the traders and bankers for the initial impulses in this remarkable development of commercial law. In Europe, as a whole, there were three new practices which led towards full negotiability. In Naples, and perhaps in Sicily, the banks began to make use of certificates of deposit that were partially negotiable. The practice developed most explicitly in Naples among the banking departments of the public pawnshops and hospitals. There is no documentary evidence prior to 1573, because the records of the banks prior to that date were destroyed by fire, but it is presumed that the practice came into use at the time of the establishment of these banking activities in 1539, or shortly after. The extended discussion of the legal attributes of these Neapolitan instruments played a vital part in the development of the Italian theories of negotiability. By analogy, this mode of transferring rights was extended to the bill of exchange in Naples and in other parts of Italy.

In the early sixteenth century, too, there appeared in France and Holland promissory notes and bills of exchange made payable to bearer. These notes and bills circulated rapidly from hand to hand, unlike the Neapolitan certificates, which were supposed to effect only one transfer. The northern practice, therefore, brought up all the major issues of negotiability. Finally, actual use of the bill of exchange was found to present some variety of circumstance. In some instances, the remittor and the presentor were the same person. At times the remittor was, in fact, the agent of the party who became the presentor. Occasionally, it was inconvenient to name the presentor when the bill was drawn, and the space was left blank, or provision made for subsequent appointment of the presentor by the inclusion of an order clause.

These various practices made bills and notes more flexible commercial instruments than was recognized by the lawyers, and the business men placed the lawyers under a positive pressure to make some provision for various problems. After much hesitation the law was made an effective instrument for the protection of the interests of business. The earliest of these legal steps that can be accurately dated is the recognition as a properly constituted agent of any bearer of bills or notes having a bearer clause. This doctrine was recognized as mercantile custom at Antwerp prior to 1535, and in 1537 it was embodied in an ordinance of Charles V. applicable to the low countries. It appears also in the statutes of Mechlen (1535), Utrecht (1550), Dordrecht (1570), and South Holland (1571). In the revised statutes of Antwerp, of 1580–81, the bearer was authorized to bring suit in his own name.

We cannot date as adequately the legal recognition of an order written on the face or the back of a document. In Italy notations of various kinds were commonly made on the face of the document, and, as a natural result, the orders of transfer of the Neapolitan certificates of deposit were written on the face of the instrument. The precise locus of these orders is a matter of indifference, and it is thus necessary to deal only with the legal content of the practice that we now properly describe as endorsement. In France and Holland orders were written on the back of the instrument. The practice is of uncertain origin, though references in Dutch treatises indicate that it became customary to note on the back any change in the relation of the parties to the original document. Thus, the appointment of a substitute by a duly constituted agent was noted on the back of the instrument of agency. It is desirable to note that the recognition of the order did not, at first, give the party any new legal rights. The party designated by the order was merely recognized as a duly constituted agent. The document thus contained all the material facts, and it ceased to be necessary to produce independent evidence of agency. These changes can be roughly identified with the second half of the sixteenth century, though the evidence is not very satisfactory in respect of dates.

The basic legal innovation is the concept of the *adjectus in rem suam* (the agent in his own affair). This new concept was first evolved in connection with various exceptional cases in respect of the bill of exchange. If the remittor and the presentor were, in fact, the same person, it was obvious that the presentor was, in truth, a principal and not an agent. Insofar as analogous cases occurred, the courts were willing to allow a party to bring forward proof that he was acting in his own behalf and not as agent for another party. Schaps holds that this curiously expressed concept laid the foundations for the modern doctrine of negotiability. The *adjectus in rem suam* could not have his agency revoked, his rights were not contingent upon the life of another, and legal procedure was instituted in his name. The doctrine appeared in Italy and in France in the late sixteenth century, but it was at first strictly limited in application.

Freundt holds that the sixteenth century merely registered progress towards full endorsement, and that only in the seventeenth century do we find positive evidence of the establishment of the new doctrines. The Neapolitan ordinance of November 8, 1607, is the earliest explicit recognition of negotiability in Italy, but it was designed to be restrictive in effect. It speaks of the inconveniences that arise in connection with several transfers, and limits the use of the order clause to a single transfer. There is a similar ordinance for Lucca in 1610, but for Venice and Florence we have evidence that such transfers were not recognized at all. It is significant, too, that even the Neapolitan legists Scaccia, Peri, and Turri ignore the emergence of the concept of negotiability. It would seem, therefore, that the new doctrine made its way very slowly, and that this unwillingness to recognize it led to the continued use of much "bearer" paper. In 1649 the commentator Laganarius recognized the endorsee as having the rights of a principal *(procurator in rem propriam),* and Italian doctrine assumed its mature form towards the close of the century in the writings of Casaregis.

In France and Holland evidence is not adequate for the first half of the seventeenth century. We have only a brief description of French practice that indicates a wide use of bearer paper. It is commonly held that bearer paper likewise dominated Dutch practice. Then, rather suddenly, endorsement was fully recognized. There is a series of ordinances at Amsterdam beginning in 1651, which establishes the basic principles of modern Dutch law, and Phoonsen, a writer on business law (1677), gave wide currency to the doctrine. In France these doctrines were embodied in the ordinance on commerce of 1673 and given wide currency by the writings of J. Savary and Bornier. The details of law and practice differ in several particulars from Italian custom, so that we may infer that the French and Dutch jurists were not entirely dependent upon the Italians, despite the priorities that appear at some points.

In Germany, several of the great fair towns attempted to prevent the introduction of endorsement, but beginning with the revised ordinance of Frankfort-am-M., September 18, 1666, legislation was favourable; but legal recognition was not general until the beginning of the eighteenth century. In England, the practice of endorsement was first described by Marius (1651), but legal recognition came only with the statutes of 1698 and 1704 (9 and 10 Will. III., c. 17; 3–4 Anne,

c. 9).[46] In Spain, the new doctrines were not fully recognized prior to the revision of commercial law embodied in the Ordinances of Bilbao in 1737.

VII

The development of the cheque and even the early advances towards negotiable paper made many changes in the details of banking practice and gradually gave deposit banking its modern aspect. These changes inevitably resulted in greater differentiation than had existed during the fifteenth century. There were wide variations in the rate of change in different localities, and the public authorities looked upon the new business practices with varying degrees of sympathy. In Naples, new practices were frankly recognized; in Venice the senate pursued an ultra–conservative policy and prohibited all change. Furthermore, general economic conditions were unfavourable to the development of trade in the Mediterranean countries. Even if there were no absolute decline, it is fairly certain that there was little growth. The banking system was thus subject to severe strains on account of the losses of commercial firms, and extensive banking failures occurred in all sections of Italy. The attempt of the authorities to meet these difficulties added appreciably to regional differentiation of banking practice.

Unfortunately, the sources available for the history of banking in the sixteenth century are not sufficiently extensive to enable us to describe conditions in Europe as a whole. For France we have only the merest indications of banking activity, and there are no unused source materials known to be available in the major public archives.[47] Much light is thrown upon conditions in the Low Countries by the activities of the great international bankers like the Fugger, and by the exchange operations of Thomas Gresham.[48] But these materials

---

[46] Richards, R. D., *The Early History of Banking in England,* London, 1929, pp. 45–46.

[47] Vigne, Marcel, *La Banque à Lyon du XVe au XVIIIe siècle,* Lyon, 1903. Although the text shows that careful use has been made of MS. material available in Lyons the description rests primarily upon printed material. The extensive bibliography includes the basic material available for France as a whole. No important MS. materials were brought to light by careful searches made by the writer in the printed inventories of the Departmental and National Archives, nor by exploratory work in Paris at the Bibliothèque Nationale and the Archives Nationales. The critical jurisdictions are the Cour des Aides and the Cour des Monnaies. The extant series are obviously very incomplete, and of the materials that would have served for work on banking only seven registers remain—Z1b, 286–90, and KK 5, 15. When and how these materials disappeared we have no means of knowing.

[48] Unwin, George, *Studies in Economic History,* London, 1927, pp. 145–67. Ehrenberg, R., *op. cit.,* II., *passim.*

have not yet furnished us with any comprehensive description of the general character of banking practice. The Fugger archives are likewise the most important single source of information for Austria and Germany, but it is, of course, important to have more knowledge of the operations of the local banking firms.[49] We are thus largely dependent upon Italian material for detailed description of banking. For many towns of the north we have only brief indications in the statutes, and the abundant material at Genoa has not been effectively utilized. Significant knowledge of detail is confined to Venice, Naples, and Sicily. In the sixteenth century, Sicily was profoundly influenced by Catalan practice, so that Catalonia and Sicily constitute together a single region. Even with these limited materials it is evident that regional differentiation became conspicuous in the course of the sixteenth century.

In Venice, the private banks were subjected to much more rigid regulation than in other parts of Italy, and towards the close of the century a new type of public bank was created whose functions were so narrowly prescribed that scarcely any use was made of credit.[50] Venice in the sixteenth century was ultra-conservative. Commissioners were appointed on June 2, 1524, to supervise the private banks, and to enforce the obligation to meet the demands of depositors. On November 6, 1526, the use of the cheque was prohibited, and some additional regulations were made. Even in Barcelona a limited use of the cheque was permitted in the Bank of Deposit, and the private bankers were allowed to use them freely. Venice alone stood out against this important development. The anxiety to make the banks safe was offset in large measure by the desire to utilize their resources for loans to the state. The amount of loans to the city was made the limit of investments in trade. Despite the reserve of 500 ducats deposited by each bank with the Commissioners under the law of 1524, the regulations failed to check the evils of excessive expansion. At all events, increasing regulation did not avert serious failures of banks. The average length of life was short, and Contarini gives the impression that practically all banks came to a bad end. This growing distrust of deposit banking led to the establishment of the famous Giro Banks: the Bank of the Rialto (1587) and the Giro Bank (1619). In 1637, the Giro Bank absorbed the Bank of the Rialto. These banks were hardly

---

[49] Jansen, Max, *Jakob Fugger der Reiche*, Leipzig, 1910. Translation by Mildred L. Hartsough, *Jacob Fugger the Rich*, New York, 1931. Reinhardt, E., *Jakob Fugger der Reiche*, Berlin, 1926. Strieder, Jakob, "Die Inventur der Firma Fugger aus dem Jahre 1527," Erganzungsheft, XVII., *Zeitschrift für die gesammte Staatswissenschaft*, 1905. Häbler, K., *Die Fugger in Spanien*, Weimar, 1897. Weitnauer, Alfred, *Venezianische Handel der Fugger*, Leipzig, 1931.

[50] Lattes, E., *op. cit., passim.* Ferrara, F., *op. cit., passim.* Dunbar, C. F., *op. cit., passim.*

more than institutions for centralized clearance; actual credit operations were prohibited. The abolition of all private banking that was originally contemplated proved to be impossible, and a number of private banks were established.

In Naples, the private banks suffered many reverses during the sixteenth century. They were subjected to some regulation, but were not as severely handled as in Venice. Beginning about 1539 with the establishment of the *Monte della Pieta,* the banks met with competition from the banking departments of these charitable foundations. The banking business was developed in order to furnish funds for the loans on pledge, or for the hospitals. The distinctive feature of these banks was the issue of certificates of deposit which were partially negotiable from an early date. They subsequently became an important element in the circulation of the region and must be recognized as the prototypes of modern credit currency. These banks also permitted the use of cheques. The *Monte della Pieta* (1539 ?) and the *Sacro Monte dei Poveri* (1563) maintained banking departments under their own name. The hospitals and charitable foundations that established banks treated their banks as separate institutions, and gave them separate names. Thus, the hospital, *Casa Santa dell' Annunciata,* established the bank *Ave Gratia Plena* in 1587. The hospital of the *Incurabili* established in 1589 the *Santa Maria del Popolo.* An orphan asylum established in 1591 the *Banco dello Spirito Sancto,* and other hospitals established the banks of *Sant Eligio* (1592), *Santi Giacomo e Vittoria* (1606), and *Santi Salvatore* (1640).[51] Although these banks have attracted little attention outside Italy, they played a more significant rôle in the history of banking than the better-known giro banks.

Sicily and Catalonia were conservative. Private banking continued with little change in the amount of regulation, but new public banks were established after the model furnished by Barcelona and Valencia. There are vague allusions to the establishment of a public bank at Trapani in 1459, but there is little evidence of an active bank. In the next century, public banks were established at Palermo (1552), Messina (1587), Gerona (1568), Saragossa, and Vich. There are general statements that would imply a much larger number of public banks in Catalonia, but particulars are not forthcoming. In general form, these banks show little modification of the original type until the first decade of the seventeenth century. Their statutes were then modified, or, as in Barcelona, a new bank was established, so that cheques could be freely used. The distinctive feature of the Catalan system was the reservation of the credit facilities of the public bank to the city and

---

[51] Tortora, Eugenio, *Nuovi documenti per la Sotoria del Banco di Napoli,* pp. 16, 17, 45, 61–62, 65–69, 82–83, 93–94, 97, Napoli, 1890.

other public authorities. The public banks acted as fiscal agents for the public authorities and supplied them with all credit needed. The private banks served the needs of trade. The contacts between public and private banks presented a number of difficult problems of policy, which were never settled in a wholly satisfactory manner. Even after the reorganization in the early seventeenth century, Catalonia and Sicily thus retained a system of pure deposit banking, modernized by the introduction of the cheque and the development of negotiable paper.

Some Suggested Readings

De Roover, Raymond A. "The Medici Bank," *Journal of Economic History* VI (1946), 24–52, 153–72; VII (1947), 69–82.

Miskimin, Harry A. "Monetary Movements and Market Structure: Forces for Contraction in Fourteenth- and Fifteenth-Century England," *Journal of Economic History,* XXIV (1964), 470–90.

Postan, Michael M. "Credit in Medieval Trade," *The Economic History Review,* I (1928), 234–61.

Usher, Abbott Payson. "Deposit Banking in Barcelona, 1300–1700," *Journal of Economic and Business History,* IV (1931), 121–55.

Plague and Economic Decline in England in the Later Middle Ages*

John Saltmarsh

As I see it, the course of English economic history in the later Middle Ages is as follows.[1] By the late thirteenth and early fourteenth centuries medieval civilization had reached a climax of material prosperity and spiritual confidence which it was never to surpass. A cessation of economic advance in the first half of the fourteenth century was followed by a positive decline in the second half, continuing and deepening in the century following, to reach its lowest point between 1450 and 1470. Recovery first started in the last twenty or twenty-five years of the fifteenth century, leading directly to the great economic renaissance which came to flowering in Tudor England. Then began that "cumulative crescendo" which was to lead, at an ever-increasing pace, through the Industrial Revolution, to the command over Nature and the vast material resources of our own day.

These are the views—or some of them—put forward by Professor Postan in a recent issue of *The Economic History Review*.[2] Professor Postan suggests that in the fifteenth century declining production was in part compensated by a more equitable distribution of the national income, with its attendant increase in social welfare. On this point I have some reservations; but everything seems to indicate a decline in total wealth, and in the whole scale of economic life in England.

It was the same elsewhere in Europe. "During the early years of the fifteenth century," wrote Pirenne, "there is observable, . . . not

---

* Reprinted from *The Cambridge Historical Journal*, Vol. VII (1941), by permission of the publisher and the author.

[1] A paper read to the Cambridge Historical Society on 5 December 1940.

[2] M. M. Postan, "The Fifteenth Century," in *The Econ[omic] Hist[ory] Rev[iew]*, IX (1939), 169.

perhaps a decline, but a cessation of all advance. Europe lived, so to speak, on what it had acquired; the economic front was stabilized."[3] The stabilized front was very evident in Germany. German colonization stopped short at the frontier of Lithuania and Latvia, was arrested in its tracks within the frontiers of Bohemia, Poland and Hungary[4]— leaving accidental, unstable, unnatural lines of division, of fatal consequence. The cessation of advance is clearly marked in the Low Countries; it can even be traced in Italy. In France, torn by foreign and civil wars fought over her territory, there was no mere stabilization, but a positive decline. Marc Bloch speaks of abandoned villages, of fields and vineyards swallowed up by the returning tide of the forest; of provinces where in a whole lifetime a man might live through nothing but imminent war; where peasants at the least alarm took refuge in woods and swamps; so that whole tracts of the kingdom were now a desolation, where "none heard crow of cock nor cluck of hen." [5]

My own observation, as far as it goes, bears out this general impression of economic decline in fifteenth-century England. Demesne land was going out of cultivation; large-scale exploitation by the lords was a thing of the past, large-scale exploitation by tenant farmers still a thing of the future. What demesnes were not abandoned were passing to the peasants on easy terms—labour services gone, rents reduced, entry fines reduced almost to nothing— or remitted altogether when the manorial court—as it often did—forced a reluctant peasant to take up a holding against his will. Tenants were hard to find in the fifteenth century, and farms a falling market; the Paston correspondence is full of complaints of rent rolls declining and tenants unwilling to continue; and on College estates it is not till the last years of the fifteenth century that any upward trend in rents can be detected. Some of the ancient customary land was also falling out of cultivation; and it is probable that on marginal lands, colonized during the period of expanding demand and high prices in the earlier Middle Ages, whole villages were being abandoned. The sands of mid-Norfolk were probably marginal in the Middle Ages; they were certainly deemed far less fertile then than they are to-day, when the foot of the sheep has turned Norfolk sand to gold, and when the barley they grow to perfection is more esteemed than the wheat they do not grow so well. Heitland's boyhood home was at Colkirk, in mid-Norfolk; and within four miles of Colkirk, he tells us in his memoirs, there were

---

[3] Henri Pirenne, *Econ[omic] and Soc[ial] Hist[ory of Medieval Europe]*, tr. I. E. Clegg (1936), 193.

[4] *Ibid.*, 194.

[5] Marc Bloch, *Les Caractères Originaux de l'Histoire Rurale Française* (1931), 118.

four ruined churches, each marking the site of an abandoned medieval village.[6] I have not seen those churches; but in the Brecklands of south-west Norfolk—marginal land in the Middle Ages, and marginal or submarginal still—I have visited five in a single afternoon. Where their ruins could be dated, they were always of the thirteenth century, and very small; the first tiny chapels built by the latest pioneer settlements of the high Middle Ages, never enlarged and early abandoned. I suspect that many, if not most of them, were abandoned before the Middle Ages ended. The arch-enemy of Tudor enclosures, John Hales himself, was of this opinion, in spite of his preoccupation with the depopulations of his own day: "the chief destruction of towns and decay of houses," he wrote in his "Defence," "was before the beginning of the reign of King Henry the Seventh."[7]

Of town life I know less; but a year or two ago I had an opportunity of examining the accounts of the Vicars Choral of York; a perpetual society of chantry priests—one might almost say, a joint-stock company—which, in return for gifts and legacies, provided masses for the souls of the citizens of that great trading centre. The endowments of the Vicars Choral consisted almost entirely in real estate within the city; they owned some 250 properties in York, including forty houses in Goodram Gate, then one of its principal commercial streets. The accounts of the Goodram Gate properties—I had no time to examine more—suggest a very serious decline in the prosperity of the city from about 1415, growing worse after 1430, and touching bottom about 1460. The aggregate fall in net revenue from the Goodram Gate properties over this period, through vacant tenements and reduced rents, was about 40%. This is an isolated instance; but Professor Postan tells us that with few exceptions—notably London—declining prosperity is evident in the bulk of English trading centres.[8]

To the men of 1349, the Great Pestilence seemed the final disaster. Friar John Clyn, the Irish Franciscan, has been quoted over and over again; but I shall quote him once more: "Lest things worthy of remembrance should perish with time, and fall away from the memory of those who are to come after us, I, seeing these many evils, and the whole world lying, as it were, in the wicked one—myself awaiting death among the dead—*inter mortuos mortem expectans*—as I have truly heard and examined, so I have reduced these things to writing; and lest the writing should perish with the writer, and the work fail together with the workman, I leave parchment for continuing the work,

---

[6] W. E. Heitland, *After Many Years* (1926), 19.

[7] "The defence of John Hales," *A Discourse of the Common Weal of this Realm of England,* ed. Lamond (1929), lxiii.

[8] Postan, *Econ. Hist. Rev.,* IX, 163.

if haply any man survive, and any of the race of Adam escape this pestilence and continue the work which I have begun."[9] Two words more he added: *magna karistia*—"great dearth"; then another hand has briefly noted—"here it seems that the author died."

The race of Adam did not perish; recovery from the first pestilence was unexpectedly rapid, and for a time life, to outward appearances, went on much as before. Yet the recovery was brief, and the lingering rot remained. From about 1360, or soon after, the serious decline set in. Slowly, but with the inexorable certainty of a hovering doom, medieval civilization died by inches. When the new age was born, it was new indeed; an age which lived increasingly for the good things of this life, increasingly lost sight of the world to come; which had forgotten the first and last principle of medieval teaching—that the only end of man on earth is that beatitude which consists in the eternal contemplation of the essence of God, and can only be attained in the life to come. In that new age men feared death chiefly in time of danger, in time of pestilence—and their fear was a keen regret for the delights and beauties of this mortal world, forever lost through the death of the body.

> Brightness falls from the air;
> Queens have died young and fair;
> Death hath closed Helen's eye;
> I am sick, I must die—
>   Lord, have mercy on us!

But the waning Middle Ages were beset with haunting terror of the hereafter; their religion held more of the fear of death everlasting than of any joys past or heavenly promise to come.

> In what state that ever I be,
>   Timor mortis conturbat me.
>
> As I me walked in one morning,
> I hard a bird both wepe and singe.
> This was the tenor of her talkinge,
>   Timor mortis conturbat me.
>
> I ask'd this birde what he meant.
> He said, I am a musket gent;
> For dred of deth I am nigh shent;
>   Timor mortis conturbat me.
>
> When I shall die know I no day,
> Therefore this songe sing I may;
> In what place or cuntrey can I not say,
>   Timor mortis conturbat me.[10]

---

[9] Charles Creighton, *Hist[ory] of Epidemics [in Britain]* (1891), I, 115.
[10] E. K. Chambers and F. Sidgwick, *Early English Lyrics* (1926), 150.

In the church of Long Melford in Suffolk, one of the last great memorials of medieval England, they wrote in black-letter above the tomb of John Clopton:

OMNIS QVI VIVIT ET CREDIT IN ME NON MORIETVR IN ETERNVM

that the men of Long Melford might worship with death ever before their eyes and in their minds; like Friar John of Kilkenny, *"inter-mortuos mortem expectans."*

This, then, is what requires explanation—no sudden collapse, but this slow, relentless decay. And this is what the sometime traditional explanation—the Black Death of 1349—signally fails to explain. Such a universal holocaust as John of Kilkenny foreboded would have been almost more credible as a consequence of the Black Death—for the mortality of 1349 was, I believe, stupendous; but the death-rate of a single year cannot explain the creeping paralysis of more than a century.

No one explanation suffices. Due weight must be allowed to the political factors—the Hundred Years' War and its aftermath, for example. Abroad, political factors were partly responsible for a contraction in English foreign trade. Not only were the continental dominions of England lost to her merchants as well as to her king; the diplomatic weakness of a land defeated in foreign war and divided by chronic civil strife assisted the successful Hansard offensive against English trade in the Baltic and Scandinavia.[11] At home, we must reckon with the depressing effects of failure to win a decisive victory—for Crécy, Poitiers and that least valuable of all famous victories, Agincourt, alike failed to win the war. We must reckon with the still more depressing effects of final defeat and the loss of the French dominions. We must reckon with heavy taxation. We must reckon also with the depredations of French privateers—and private pirates too, many of them rascally Englishmen mischievously fishing in the troubled Channel waters; with Scottish incursions, and Continental descents on the English coasts—witness the Flemish raid on Norfolk described by Margaret Paston.[12] All this did moral as well as material damage; a nation can be excused war-weariness when the war lasts a hundred years. The brutalization of the country by the gangsterdom of returned soldiers is a familiar theme; the breakdown of law and order at home equally familiar. English government had been weak before, but never, perhaps, since Stephen's reign, had the breakdown been so complete, nor even then so prolonged.

Due weight must be given to the personal factor: royal minorities,

---

[11] Cf. M. M. Postan in *English Trade in the Fifteenth Century* 123, 131, 136.
[12] *Paston Letters,* ed. James Gairdner (1910), 1, 42.

weak kings and quarrelsome uncles; an age barren in political talent, among kings and ministers alike. England found no Philip the Good or Louis the Eleventh.

To other factors less weight may be allowed. Pirenne's theory of class war provoked by an increasingly rigid and burdensome social system[13] does not fit the facts of English society—though true enough, no doubt, in Flanders and elsewhere. Apart from the revolt of 1381, class warfare was almost wholly absent in England at this time, for its causes were absent. English urban society seems to have preserved the career open to talents more successfully than Flanders did[14]— perhaps because capitalistic industry in England was more backward than across the Narrow Seas; and the cessation of colonization which limited the opportunities of the continental peasant[15] actually, I believe, lightened the burdens of the husbandmen of England.

The once-popular theory of soil exhaustion—the alleged result of centuries of over-cropping and insufficient manuring under the open-field system—need no longer be taken seriously. There is not, and never was, a shred of evidence to support it that will bear criticism, and scientific probability, to put it mildly, is against it.

To the famines and murrains of the early fourteenth century only a limited temporary importance need be attached. There had been severe famines before 1315—in 1194, for instance, and in 1257—and they had not arrested the flood-tide of expanding medieval economy. And from murrains, in particular, the sheep population of England, with its frequent generations, could recover very rapidly. Natural disasters, such as floods, probably possessed a limited local importance. Some fertile lands were drowned; some flourishing ports were engulfed, like Dunwich and Ravenser, or slowly silted up, like Hedon and Chester; but England remained. And, once again, isolated disasters do not explain prolonged decay; though, incidentally, political dry-rot and recurrent warfare may do so very well.

But the very nature of the decline suggests another cause at work— a falling population. Professor Postan suggests it as a probable explanation;[16] some of the symptoms which I have already mentioned— contracting cities, deserted villages—suggest it strongly, and so does an examination of English agrarian conditions. The thirteenth century was an age of land hunger, but the fifteenth was an age of what I call, for want of a better name, land surfeit. In the thirteenth century lords were extending their demesnes, and peasants, wherever they could,

---

[13] Pirenne, *Econ. and Soc. Hist.*, 196 et seq.
[14] Cf. Pirenne, *Econ. and Soc. Hist.*, 202.
[15] *Ibid.*, 196–97.
[16] Postan, *Econ. Hist. Rev.*, IX, 166.

were extending their holdings, by intakes from the waste; lords were demanding increased labour services, and peasants were paying them. The demand of lords and peasants for more land, the demand of lords for more labour, the acquiescence of peasants in heavier services— all, I believe, can readily be explained in terms of rising population in the prosperous high Middle Age. Peasants wanted more land because the village had more mouths to feed and more hands to keep busy. Lords wanted more land because rising population meant a rising demand for agricultural produce, and rising demand meant rising prices and rising profits. Lords wanted heavier services because an extension of the demesne called for more labour to till it; and peasants agreed to them because they could not face the alternative: eviction, and a hopeless quest for another holding. For suppose they refused; the lord had no difficulty in finding a new tenant. Ready to his hand stood the younger sons of the village—that same reserve which was still in the background in 1349 to step into the places of those who fell in the Pestilence. But the peasant would have great difficulty in finding fresh land to till. This may seem a paradox, in an England that still abounded in waste and wild. But there were at least two decisive limiting factors—the one legal, the other economic. In the first place, the waste did not stand open to any man to till; it was—as it still is—the private property of the lord of the manor, and his permission must be sought before an assart could be made. Lords would not give facilities on the waste to their own evicted peasants; nor were tenants so hard to come by that they would willingly entertain—as in a later age and quite contrary conditions—the run-away peasants of another manor. The economic factor was probably still more decisive. The desert does not blossom in a day, and untilled waste, even if you can get it, is a very different commodity from land long cultivated and in good heart. To create a holding out of manorial waste required capital, and, still more, time; and while land was being broken up and made productive, the evicted peasant would starve. Peasant assarting—the new capital investment of the medieval village— must at all times have proceeded from the firm base of an established enterprise, by slow and piecemeal means; an acre or two added, at intervals of years, to a holding which was already supporting its holder, which left him a margin of working days, over and above the toil required to keep body and soul together, in which to break up fresh land. To start an entirely new agricultural enterprise on virgin soil, without an assured livelihood for a season or two from other sources, was quite out of the question.

So in the thirteenth century cultivated land was in short supply, and strongly held, just because men were plentiful and men were at a discount. To the modern Gradgrind's dream of two men for

every job corresponded then the actuality of the grasping lord's ideal—
two tenants for every holding.

We have already seen that agrarian conditions in the waning Middle
Ages were far otherwise. Now cultivated land was in redundant supply,
and it was no longer strongly held. Lords eager to let, ready even to
abandon; peasants prepared to desert their holdings,[17] counting them no
longer worth services or rents fixed in days when the land market
was still brisk—all this is inconceivable in the thirteenth century, or
for that matter in the sixteenth. Tenants wooed by rent reductions,
free labourers by rising real wages—this is just as inconceivable in
any age of land hunger and plentiful labour supply. Now there were
no longer two tenants for every holding, but—often in the most literal
sense—two holdings for every tenant. The secular balance of land
and men had swung over, so that men were at a premium, land now
at a discount.

In the absence of technical improvements (of which there is no
evidence) the change implies a shift in the balance between the land
available for cultivation and the men available and eager to cultivate
it. The land did not, and could not, of itself increase; the shift must
have been in demand, not in supply. There are no statistics; but the
symptoms of the fifteenth-century land market suggest the diagnosis
of a falling population as strongly as thirteenth-century land hunger
suggests a population that was rising. Moreover, the symptoms of
the fifteenth century suggest a continuous fall over a long period;
not simply a population that had fallen, but one which was falling
progressively; not by one sudden disaster, but by a long-drawn-
out attrition.

Where is the cause of such an attrition to be sought? It must be a
cause which was not at work in the expansive days of the thirteenth
century, nor probably before the second half of the fourteenth. It
must persist throughout the greater part of the fifteenth century,
slackening sufficiently in the sixteenth to permit of renewed expansion.
It must be powerful enough, while at its height, to constitute a steady
and important drain on the population of England. The Black Death
of 1349, standing alone, will not fill the bill; but a permanent infection
of England by a new and fatal disease will fill it very well.

The Black Death was undoubtedly plague properly so called—
plague in the medical sense. The habits of plague are very remarkable.
As a permanent member of the family of human diseases, its prevalence is extremely local. Its home is in certain limited regions where
it is continually recurring, either in sporadic cases or local epidemics.

---

[17] *Cf.* F. W. Maitland, "History of a Cambridgeshire Manor," in *Collected
Papers* (1911), II. 401.

Such foci are found in Uganda, in Western Arabia, in Kurdistan, northern India and the region of the Gobi Desert.[18] For centuries together, plague may never be seen outside these small districts. And then, at rare intervals, it ceases its home-keeping habits, and sets out on the march. It spreads relentlessly, but not very rapidly—not nearly so rapidly, for instance, as influenza, which is here to-day and all over the country next week. Pandemic plague may take several years to circle the earth; but it spreads far, it strikes hard, and it comes to stay. These periodical pandemics, with the plague periods which they inaugurate, are believed to have a common characteristic historical form. At the first onset—as with many new diseases—there is very great mortality, and it is spread, though not evenly, over an immense area, in town and country alike. Then follows the aftermath—a prolonged period, perhaps centuries long, of endemic plague on a small scale, and of recurring epidemics, first general and then local—often severe, though not to be compared in severity with the first attack. Towards the end of the plague period, the intervals between outbreaks seem to grow longer, and for the most part they are limited to the towns, especially the larger towns; with a few unimportant exceptions, the countryside is free. The pattern of a plague period may be compared to that of a fire which sweeps through a forest with a mighty blaze; dies down, but leaves behind it patches of smouldering undergrowth, which from time to time break out into fresh flames; as times goes on, the flames break out more rarely, the smaller patches of smouldering ash grow cold; at last even the largest are extinct, and the fire, like the plague, is gone.

The detailed evidence of this pattern is drawn from one plague period only, for no more than three are known to recorded history, and of these, one is remote and little known, and the evidence for another is still incomplete. The first began with the plague of Justinian; the second with the Black Death; the third with the pandemic of 1896—and in that plague period we are living to-day.

The first pandemic probably spread outwards from one of the Near Eastern foci; it broke out in Egypt in 542.[19] It passed through the whole Roman Empire, and probably reached England—certainly it reached Ireland—soon after its outbreak in Byzantium. For at least a hundred years there seems to have been plague infection in the British Isles; in 664 there was a great pestilence which can be identified as plague—again from Irish records. Thereafter there is plenty of evidence of epidemics in medieval Britain, but no record of the characteristic symptoms of plague. By 1349 the infection of Justinian's pandemic must have been long extinct in this country.

---

[18] M. Greenwood, *Epidemics and Crowd Diseases* (1935), 290.
[19] Creighton, *Hist. of Epidemics,* I, 159.

The second pandemic has a long and well-documented history. Most of us think only of two great outbreaks of plague in modern English history: the Black Death, and the so-called "Great Plague of London." In reality the case is otherwise. The London plague of 1665 is remembered not because it was the greatest but because it was the last London plague, separated by an interval of fifteen years from preceding serious outbreaks in the city, an interval of forty years from the last catastrophic epidemic. The mortality, in proportion to total population, was perhaps less severe than in 1625;[20] probably no more severe than in many London plagues of earlier date. Nor— in the first century or two following 1349—were provincial cities free; the countryside itself suffered in national epidemics in the later fourteenth century, from local infection in the fifteenth. The Paston Letters speak of plague in a Norfolk village in the 1460's.[21] Even in years when there was no epidemic, sporadic cases of plague might be common in the towns. In 1580 there were only 128 deaths in London; so Creighton calls it a year "almost clear" of plague.[22] In all the three centuries following the Black Death, plague smouldered continually in every city, flared up ever and anon. But by the end of the seventeenth century it was extinct in England, and everywhere in Europe, except Russia. There it lingered a generation or two longer.

The pandemic of 1896 has an important history outside Europe. It really began in 1892, or earlier, in Yunnan. In 1894 it reached Canton and Hongkong, in 1896 it reached Bombay.[23] From these sea-ports it spread around the world, and many of the centres of infection which it established are still in existence. Every Indian province was infected by 1898. In California, in Madagascar, in Hawaii, in the Azores, in the Dutch East Indies and various foci in South America, it has been active within the last ten or twelve years.[24] But in England, as elsewhere in Europe, it signally failed to take root. It made its appearance in England, certainly in 1910, probably as early as 1906, in a tiny corner of Suffolk—the narrow tongue of land between the Orwell and the Stour. But it never spread; it caused less than a score of deaths; and it seems to have died out by about 1918.[25]

The explanation of this periodic character of plague lies in the fact that it is primarily a rodent infection,[26] and especially an infection

---

[20] See estimated figures in Creighton, *op. cit.*, I, 660.
[21] Quoted *ibid.*, I, 226.
[22] *Ibid.*, I, 345.
[23] Greenwood, *Epidemics and Crowd Diseases*, 296.
[24] H. H. Scott, *History of Tropical Medicine* (1939), II, 724.
[25] Greenwood, *op. cit.*, 294.
[26] H. H. Scott, *op. cit.*, II, 742.

of wild rodents living remote from man. *Pasteurella pestis,* the causative organism, is a parasite with two hosts, insect and animal—living alternately in the blood stream of an animal and the stomach of a flea, and transferred from one animal host to another by the flea's bite. Man will serve as an animal host; but the animal host *par excellence* is a rodent. It is among wild rodent species of the prairie and the forest that plague is permanently endemic. In these centres of so-called sylvatic, or forest, plague, the infection is never extinct; here, in the periods between human epidemics, the organism of plague lives in the blood of wild rodents, passing from infected to non-infected by the agency of fleas. Occasionally a human comes into contact with an infected wild rodent, is bitten by one of its infected fleas: these are the sporadic human cases which occur, outside the pandemic period, among those who live in the permanently infected regions.

In the great pandemics, the infection is carried, chiefly on board ship, from one of the endemic centres far and wide over the world. Thereafter, it is kept alive in numerous centres by rats. Even in pandemic periods, it is only among rats or other rodents that plague smoulders in the off-season, and the probability of its survival in a village or town increases with the size of the town.[27] Hence its limitation to fewer and fewer centres throughout the fifteenth and sixteenth centuries; but other factors probably contributed to its final disappearance from England after 1665. All these factors seem to have acted in the same way—by reducing the risk which humans run of being bitten by an infected flea. First of all, the greater cleanliness of houses, as well as greater personal cleanliness, has reduced the number of fleas living in close association with humans. The straw-strewn floors and the straw bedding of medieval England must have provided lurking places for countless fleas. Secondly, the increasing proportion of brick-built houses, in place of houses of wood or of mud-and-stud, has rendered human dwellings less desirable homes for rats. Bricks cannot be gnawed.[28] But more important than either of these, in all probability, was the complete change in the rat population.[29] Some time around the end of the seventeenth century, England was invaded—by the brown rat, sewer rat, *Rattus norvegicus,* or, in contemporary language, the Hanover rat. The brown rat is a more powerful animal, and a better fighter, than *Rattus rattus,* the black rat of medieval England. *Rattus rattus* was exterminated, for the brown rat beat him every time to the available food supplies—and among rats the iron law of Malthus holds in all its rigidity; where reproduction

[27] Greenwood, *op. cit.,* 300.
[28] H. H. Scott, *op. cit.,* II, 735.
[29] H. H. Scott, *loc. cit.*

proceeds at such a rate, population is always limited by the means of subsistence, and the weakest goes to the wall. Only on shipboard the black rat held his own; though a worse fighter, he is a better climber, and on board ship that counts for quite a lot. Most of us have little love for the brown rat; but for two important reasons he is a less dangerous neighbour than *Rattus rattus*. He does not usually share human dwellings; he prefers to live out of doors, and comes into houses chiefly on midnight foraging expeditions; so the fleas which live in his nest are less likely to find their way into human beds and human clothing. Moreover, every species of rat has its own peculiar species of flea; and among rat fleas tastes differ. All prefer rats; but while some are quite ready to bite a human if no rat offers, others will do so only in the very last resort. Some of the black rat's fleas will bite a human fairly readily; but the brown rat's fleas bite humans only under extreme provocation. For both these reasons, the expulsion of the black rat by the brown greatly reduced the risk of human infection.

Lastly, there is the ancient explanation of the Great Fire of London, which doubtless destroyed many thousands of rats and countless fleas, and may thus have abruptly broken the chain of infection in the principal focus of plague in England.

Two of our conditions are satisfied. The plague was a new factor in population movements, not at work before 1349. Its force slackened with time, especially after the later fifteenth century—as will appear in more detail in a later paragraph; and after 1665 it ceased to be a factor at all. If we can assume that its effects were serious in relation to population and birth-rate, then we may conclude that plague must have had a peculiar retarding influence on population movements in late medieval England, distinguishing the period from those by which it was preceded and followed.

How serious was mortality from plague? Naturally, no exact answer can be given; we do not know the figures for the population or the birthrate, or the general rate of mortality from plague. But there is good evidence, if only for a narrow field, for the fourteenth century and the sixteenth, and some indication for the critical fifteenth century.

A great deal of statistical material survives for a study of the mortality in the year of the Black Death itself; but its preparation involves great labour, and much of the work done upon it has been rendered useless by insufficient critical examination. I have used four collections of statistics (though no doubt there are others) which seem absolutely trustworthy: those of Professor Hamilton Thompson, Miss F. M. Page, Mr. Ballard and Father Etienne Robo.

Let me say at once that I can see no ground for minimizing the mortality in this first pestilence. The testimony is staggering. Miss Page, Mr. Ballard and Father Robo all work in limited fields, and all deal with a selected class—manorial tenants. In three Cambridgeshire villages Miss Page records a mortality of 47% at Dry Drayton, 57% at Cottenham, and 70% at Oakington.[30] In the Hundred of Farnham in Surrey, Father Robo finds that over 300 tenants died under the Great Pestilence—the death roll was fifteen times normal in 1348–9, and ten times normal in 1349–50;[31] figures that mean something. At Witney in Oxfordshire and at Downton in Hampshire Mr. Ballard finds that about two-thirds of the tenants died. Only at Brightwell in Berkshire was the mortality less—there, according to Mr. Ballard, it was about one-third, and even that is quite enough.[32]

Professor Hamilton Thompson's geographical field is far from narrow.[33] The two dioceses of Lincoln and York covered between them something like a quarter of the area (though probably a good deal less than a quarter of the population) of fourteenth-century England. Lincoln included nearly the whole of the counties of Lincolnshire, Leicestershire, Rutland, Northamptonshire, Buckinghamshire, Oxfordshire, Huntingdonshire, Bedfordshire and Hertfordshire; York, the whole counties of Yorkshire and Nottinghamshire, and parts of Lancashire, Westmorland and Cumberland. Here, between Thames and Tees, Professor Thompson has collected and carefully criticized the figures for all the benefices to which the two diocesans had institution—well over 2000. In the twelve months from Lady Day, 1349, to Lady Day, 1350, about 41% were vacant by death. The percentage for the diocese of Lincoln is 40.17%;[34] that for York 44.22%;[35] but the figures for the several deaneries vary greatly. Percentages of 60 and over are found around Lincoln itself, on the banks of the Humber and the Thames, and in a Yorkshire coastal area between Scarborough and Driffield. In the Deanery of Hitchin, on the other hand, the figure was little over 15%; in half-a-dozen others it was under 25%. Mortality was notably light in the Fens—Holland and St. Ives are among the deaneries with under 25% of deaths among the beneficed clergy[36]—and in moorland deaneries such as Cleveland.

---

[30] F. M. Page, *Estates of Crowland Abbey* (1934), 123.

[31] Etienne Robo, *Medieval Farnham* (1935), 212.

[32] A. Ballard, *The Black Death,* in Oxford Studies in Social and Legal History, Vol. V (1916).

[33] A. Hamilton Thompson, "Registers of John Gynewell, Bishop of Lincoln, for the years 1347–1350," *Arch[aeological] Journal,* LXVIII (1911), 301 *et seq.;* "The Pestilences of the Fourteenth Century in the Diocese of York," *ibid.,* LXXI (1914), 97 *et seq.*

[34] *Arch. Journal,* LXVIII, 316.

[35] Based on tables in *Arch. Journal,* LXXI, 129–31.

[36] Mortality was also light in the marshy districts of Yorkshire, *Arch. Journal,* LXXI, 112–13.

A careful correlation of the figures, district by district, with the variations in settlement and economic life, would be of great interest. It would probably show that mortality was greatest where the rat population was densest—that is to say, where food for rats was most plentiful: first in the towns and especially the seaports and riverports; then in the fertile corn-growing districts; and lightest in pastoral and thinly settled areas.

Variations in the incidence of the mortality are sometimes used as an argument for minimizing its severity; although some districts suffered heavily, it is said, others, about which we know less, were probably less affected; and the known figures give a false impression of the general average. I do not think this argument holds. In the first place, the evidence is geographically fairly widely spread, and the selection is thoroughly at random—if anything biassed against the most populous regions, including some—such as the Bristol region—where we know the plague was especially severe. Secondly, the evidence suggests that the districts which escaped lightly were just those which carried least weight in the general average of population and were of least importance in economic life—those which were thinly peopled and remote.

It is often argued that the beneficed clergy underwent special risks in visiting the sick, and that mortality among them was correspondingly high. This, I think, can well be exaggerated. First, their number included, as an offset, those wealthy non-residents whom Professor Thompson shows to have been especially successful in avoiding infection. Secondly, in the bubonic form of plague, the risk of infection is not so closely connected with the person of the human patient as in the case of most other epidemics; it is dispersed wherever infected rats and fleas abound.[37] The poor in general, and all who lived in contact with these creatures, were almost equally at risk with the most assiduous of the clergy. The way of escape was not to avoid the sickroom, but to avoid the stricken house, the stricken street, the stricken town; nothing short of evacuation was of any avail. Evacuation was open to the fortunately circumstanced—the companions of the Decameron and University scholars, for example; but not to the poor; and the poor—including peasants and craftsmen—were the great bulk of the population. They partook by necessity and continuously of the same risk which the good priest accepted of choice but intermittently. It is worth noting that the figures for manorial tenants agree fairly closely with those for the beneficed clergy.

---

[37] This is because bubonic plague can only be contracted through the bite of a flea, and not by direct contact with the human sufferer. The far more deadly pneumonic form, on the other hand, is conveyed by personal contact; as for example in the very fatal outbreaks in Manchuria.

From the point of view of age and sex, both manorial tenants and beneficed clergy are of course not representative of the population—especially the latter, who were wholly male, almost wholly adult, and perhaps preponderantly somewhat more advanced in years than even the general adult population. For this age-group we might perhaps expect a normal death-rate rather above the average; but the effect of this on the figures is negligible. Normal mortality among the beneficed clergy of York and Lincoln was at the rate of 3½% to 4%;[38] deduct this from 41%, and the severity of plague mortality appears hardly less.

Taking everything into consideration, I should not be surprised to learn that a third of the population, or even more, perished in 1349. That the manorial system recovered so rapidly—in the sense that new tenants were so readily found to take the place of the old—I should attribute to a previous redundance of population and labour. Fourteenth-century villages were probably full of land-hungry younger sons, squatters and labourers and poor relations living, and toiling for their living, on a family farm; and these would be only too ready to take up a vacant holding.

It is perhaps a coincidence that the beginnings of the permanent decay of the manorial system can first be traced, here and there, about the time of the second plague—the Pestis Secunda of 1361. Perhaps a coincidence—though one can well imagine the formidable moral effect of recurring plagues. One great disaster, if once over and done with, may be followed by confident recovery; a disaster that recurs and recurs again is far more discouraging—not merely a disaster, but a stupid and tedious bore.

Like the plague of 1349, and unlike the plagues of the sixteenth century, these outbreaks of the later fourteenth seem to have been general and not local. The death-rate was of course far less than in 1349; yet it might well be less, and still have a serious effect on population. Professor Thompson has compiled statistics for the diocese of York in 1361, 1362 and 1369, and for part of the diocese of Lincoln in 1361. In 1361 and 1362 the diocese of York escaped lightly, with a mortality of about 6.2% in each year. Mortality was heavier in 1369—about 13.4%, or between three and four times the normal figure. Further south, mortality in 1361 seems to have been

---

[38] In the diocese of Lincoln (excluding the Lincoln archdeaconry, for which figures are not available) 72 benefices out of a total of 1304 were vacant by death in the 18 months from 23 September 1347 to 24 March 1348–49—a yearly average of about 3.7% (*Arch. Journal*, LXVIII, 316, n. 1; 335–8). In the diocese of York, 24 out of 536 benefices were vacant by death in the 15 months ending 24 March 1348–49—a yearly average of about 3.6% (*Arch. Journal*, LXXI, 129–31).

heavier still. The archdeaconries of Lincoln and Stowe (approximating to the county of Lincoln) give a figure of about 11%—about three times normal; but for the archdeaconries of Leicester and Northampton the figure is about 23½ %, or about six times normal.[39] Mortality such as this is not to be despised; if it is general, and recurs regularly at intervals of seven or eight years, it is quite powerful enough to convert a natural increase of population into a natural decrease. I suggest that these later epidemics may well have been responsible for a continuous decline of population in the later fourteenth century.

Similar figures for the fifteenth century are lacking. Plagues were of frequent occurrence; but for the rate of mortality I know of only one scrap of evidence—Creighton's conclusion based on the obituary of the monastery of Canterbury, that between 1349 and 1517 one-third of the deaths among monks were due to plague;[40] a suggestive scrap, but not enough to build upon.

In default of more, I turn to the century following. The London bills of mortality were instituted in 1532.[41] The Court suspected that the citizens were concealing plague in their midst, for fear London should be deserted by the King and nobles—paying customers. The government therefore required weekly returns to be made. The earlier bills have survived only in fragments; but for the five years 1578–82 the series is very nearly complete.[42] The bills show separately deaths from plague, deaths from other causes and—very fortunately for our purpose—births. Admittedly, the collection of these statistics left much to be desired. Diagnosis was carried out, we are told, by ignorant old women. But the plague was very easy to know and recognize, and the ignorant old women had plenty of experience. Moreover, it was very inconvenient to have a plague death in the house—seclusion followed, the scarlet cross, Lord have mercy upon us and all the rest of it; to say nothing of the serious risk which the secluded survivors ran of themselves dying of the disease. As a sanitary precaution, seclusion was far worse than useless. Fortunately it was unpopular; fortunately bribery could sometimes avert it; and the scales were therefore weighted—as far as bribery and other means of persuasion weighed with ignorant old women—against the plague diagnosis. The figures strongly suggest that persuasion was often effective. Deaths from other causes increase suspiciously in plague-years; it is pretty clear that many plague-deaths were being certified as due to some cause other

---

[39] *Arch. Journal*, LXXI, 115–16. The figures for the diocese of Lincoln are stated by Professor Hamilton Thompson to be based on a rough calculation, subject to future revision.

[40] Creighton, *Hist. of Epidemics*, I, 226.

[41] *Ibid.*, I, 294.

[42] *Ibid.*, I, 341.

than plague. The bills of mortality, therefore, probably underestimate the effect of plague on the death-roll.

The London statistics have this great advantage over those of the fourteenth century—that they apply to a balanced community of every age and sex. They have this disadvantage—that we do not know the total population of London in 1578, and so cannot calculate the percentage rate. But we have the total of births, which is much more valuable.

The years 1578–82 included two epidemics—in the first and the last years of the series; two years when plague was at endemic level—1579 and 1581; one, 1580, which was exceptionally free of infection. In the whole period about 24,800 deaths are recorded; about 8300—almost exactly one-third—are entered as plague-deaths. For the reasons I have just given, this proportion is almost certainly an underestimate—perhaps by as much as 2000. Forty per cent of total deaths due to plague is quite a probable figure.

But the figures for deaths are most instructive by comparison with the figures for births. The year 1580 was almost clear of plague. There were 3568 births, 2873 deaths—a net increase of 695. It was rather a prolific year; births were about 155 above the five-year average; but had they been no more than the average, there would still have been an increase of 540. Now take the average annual figure for births and deaths over the whole five years—3413 births, 5109 deaths—a net annual decrease of 1696. It is a reasonable conclusion that plague converted the movement of London's population from a small natural increase to a considerably larger natural decrease.

This does not mean, of course, that the population of London was actually declining. On the contrary, it was almost certainly expanding; the natural decrease was more than compensated by immigration.

I regard these London figures as much the most significant evidence that we have; and in the light of these figures I propose to re-examine what is known of plague in the fifteenth century. First it must be admitted that plagues were rather more frequent in 1578–82 than was usual in the late sixteenth century; the average interval between serious epidemics was then about six years. But even if we omit one of the two epidemic years, and take a four-year average, there is still an annual decrease of 1200 or 1300. And in all five years, 1580 is the only one in which births were in excess of deaths.

In the fifteenth century, plagues were if anything rather more frequent; in London there were at least twenty to twenty-four outbreaks in a hundred years. What is more significant, there were two very unhealthy periods in mid-century. Between 1433 and 1454 there were eight or nine plague-years in London—eight or nine out of twenty-one. A lull followed; but in 1462 a Cambridge boy, walking by the front gate of the Old Court of King's, met an old man with a beard, who addressed him thus: "Go now and tell to any one that within these two years there will be such pestilence and famine, and slaughter of men, as no man living has seen." Thereupon the old man disappeared. Doubts were cast on the veracity of the boy; but the old man's words came true. There was plague in London in 1464; in 1465; in 1467; in 1471; in 1474; the worst plagues of all in 1478 and 1479—plague epidemics in every second year for sixteen years.[43] If the effect of a plague-year on population in the fifteenth century was anything like what it was in the late sixteenth, the effect on London's prosperity in these two periods must have been very great.

I have taken London as an example, because London's history is better documented in this period. But other towns had their plague-years; not necessarily the same years as London's, but sufficiently frequent—witness the thirty dispersals of Oxford in the fifteenth century. Moreover, it is probable that some of the greater plagues still affected the whole country, or at least all the principal towns, almost simultaneously. Hull, Newcastle and Norwich all shared the London epidemics of 1478 and 1479. Creighton believes that the plague of 1407, and possibly that of 1439, swept through all England. In 1471 the younger Sir John Paston wrote: "I cannot hear by pilgrims, . . . nor none other man that rideth or goeth any country, that any borough town in England is free of that sickness. God cease it when it please him!"[44]

The London figures for 1578–82 show how a succession of plague epidemics could revolutionize population movements. There was such a succession of epidemics in England, on a national scale from 1361 to some point in the fifteenth century; thereafter on a local scale, and restricted to the towns, and especially to the greater towns. From the middle of the sixteenth century the frequency of plagues grew less in London—probably this happened earlier in smaller centres of population. More than any single catastrophe, this continual sapping of the human resources of England would account for the gradual but continuous decay of her prosperity. The fact that mortality was heaviest in the most highly organized centres of economic life would make its effects all the more felt—would perhaps provide an additional reason for the migration of industry to the rural safe areas, and the decay of the ancient towns. The period in the middle of the fifteenth century which was—if we may judge by London—especially unhealthy, coincides with the deepest point of the depression; and the gradual slackening of the power of plague, which naturally sets in as its reign

---

[43] Creighton, op. cit., I, 225 et seq.
[44] Quoted ibid., I, 230.

wears on, would permit the gradual recovery of the early Tudor period. The great disaster of the Black Death has distracted the attention of historians from the later and lesser epidemics of plague; but these, in their cumulative effect, may well explain more in English history than the Black Death itself.

This is admittedly a theory based far more on inference than on evidence; therefore it remains a theory; nor does it claim to be more than one among many possible explanations. But it is necessary to bear in mind that epidemic disease has more power over human life than famine, flood or tempest, let alone the march of armies or the policy of kings; that of all epidemic diseases, plague is the most deadly and the most demoralizing; that plague haunted the closing Middle Age in England, while the period before, and the period in which medieval history has been written, were wholly free from its menace. There is but one way of entering the world; the ways of leaving it are countless. Add to all the rest this last and greatest risk of death, and there is small wonder that the Middle Age dragged out its final years in gloom and decay.

Some Suggested Readings

Bean, J. M. W. "Plague, Population and Economic Decline in England in the Later Middle Ages," *The Economic History Review*, XV (1963), 423–37.

Herlihy, David. "Population, Plague and Social Change in Rural Pistoia, 1201–1430," *The Economic History Review*, XVIII (1965), 225–44.

Lipson, Ephraim. "The Black Death," *Economic Journal*, XXVII (1917), 78–86.

Power, E. E. "Historical Revisions: VII—The Effects of the Black Death on Rural Organization in England," *History*, III (1918), 110–16.

Robbins, Helen. "A Comparison of the Effects of the Black Death on the Economic Organization of France and England," *Journal of Political Economy*, XXXVI (1928), 447–79.

The Fifteenth Century*

Michael M. Postan

Few periods of English economic history have been so much misunderstood by writers of general histories as the fifteenth century. The fault is partly the researcher's, who until very recently fought shy of the economic history of the period. Yet much more is now known to specialists than has penetrated the consciousness of the general historians. In text-books and political surveys the economic history of the fifteenth century is still made up of a few conventions for which recent research offers no justification.

The conventional notions die so hard, simply because they appear to fit into general preconceptions about the period. Coming as it does at the very end of what is regarded as the Middle Ages and just before the Tudor era, the century is easy to interpret as one of "transition": as a time during which the so-called medieval development was completed and the great Tudor achievement prepared. And people who view the whole of English economic history as a continuous ascent from the barbaric primitivity of the pre-conquest days to the glorious efflorescence of the renaissance, find an easy explanation of the fifteenth century in its position between the fourteenth and the sixteenth. It is easy to assume, as most textbooks in fact do assume, that everything which the sixteenth century possessed—industrial and commercial expansion, mercantile capital, middle classes, agricultural progress, enclosures—was to be found in the fifteenth century in a degree somewhat smaller than in the sixteenth though somewhat greater than in the fourteenth.

This reading of the economic history of the age as one of "transition" was at one time very nearly upset by the much advertised conflict of views between Denton and Thorold Rogers. While Denton brought out the deterioration of economic life during the Wars of the Roses

* Reprinted from *The Economic History Review*, Vol. IX (1938–39), by permission of the publisher and the author.

Thorold Rogers stressed the prosperity of the peasantry, and it fell to Kingsford to reconcile the conflict and to confuse the issue by arguing that the period being one of transition was bound to have a chequered record, and that its economic and political achievements were broken by intermittent light and shade, or as he preferred to describe it, "prejudice and promise."[1] Yet had the hints contained in Denton and Rogers been followed up and the contradiction explored, a truer reading might have emerged. A further investigation of Denton's views would have revealed how little the economic development of the fifteenth century owed to its being sandwiched between the fourteenth and the sixteenth, and would have shown it not as a century of growth but as an age of recession, arrested economic development and declining national income. At the same time an investigation of Rogers's views would have shown that their contradiction to those of Denton was only an apparent one. For whereas Denton's pessimistic reading applied to the economic development of the country as a whole, Rogers's applied to the well-being of the lower ranks of rural society. That for a time a relative decline in the total volume of national wealth is fully compatible with the rising standard of life of the labouring classes is a proposition which students of post-war England will find it easy to understand. And that this is what in fact happened we shall presently see.

I

That the total national income and wealth was declining is shown by almost every statistical index available to historians. Most of these are indirect, but they are sufficiently unanimous to leave no room for doubt.

The most direct and the most important are the indices of agricultural production. That the cultivation of the demesne, the manorial home-farm, was declining throughout the century has always been known to historians, and the decline has always been accounted for by the changing organisation of the manor, i.e. the substitution of peasant leases for the direct cultivation of the demesne. But in the light of more recent study it appears that the reorganisation of agriculture was not the only cause of the drop in manorial production. The falling figures of manorial yields reflect not only the letting out of the demesne but also a real decline in agriculture. On most of the estates for which the evidence is available, more land was withdrawn from

---

[1] C. L. Kingsford, *Prejudice and Promise in XVth Century England*, pp. 64–77; Thorold Rogers, *History of Agriculture and Prices*, Vol. V, pp. 3–5, 23; W. Denton, *England in the Fifteenth Century*, pp. 115, 118, 119.

the demesne than was let out to tenants. In other words there was a net contraction of the area under cultivation.

The impression of contraction is further supported by what we learn of the area actually occupied by peasant tenants. From the fifties and sixties of the fourteenth century right until the last quarter of the fifteenth ominous entries of vacant lands, *"terre in manu domini,"* appear in manorial accounts; and the number of vacant holdings and lapsed rents grow continually throughout the period. True enough, not all the lands which reverted to the lord after the pestilences of the fourteenth century or in the course of the fifteenth century remained permanently vacant, for some of them were re-let to new tenants, mostly on lease. But even if we make all the allowances for the new re-lettings there still remains a constantly growing deficiency both in the area of customary land in the hands of the tenants and in its total yield of rent. Of the 450 odd manors for which the fifteenth-century accounts have been studied, over four hundred show a contraction of land in the hands of tenants, and a corresponding fall in rents.[2]

The general impression is therefore one of a slack demand for land, and a relatively abundant supply of holdings. This impression is reinforced by what we learn of the petering out of reclamations—the assarts and purprestures. Although it would be wrong to think that the taking in of new land ceased altogether—in fact in some parts of the country, such as the weald of Sussex or the woodlands of Herts and Bucks, it was quite active throughout the fifteenth century—the great colonising effort of the earlier age is definitely over. At its most active the new reclamation is a matter of odd acres or perches here and there, carved out of the waste by individual peasant tenants. Nowhere do we find large tracts broken up and colonised on a scale comparable to the great colonising ventures of the late twelfth and the thirteenth centuries.

It is therefore no wonder that the values of land, however measured, were falling off. The vacant customary holdings fetched lower rents when let out by the lords to leaseholders than they had done in the hands of the customary tenants. In many places both customary and leasehold rents had to be scaled down to suit the new situation. Entry fines which on some estates had soared up to unprecedented heights during the great land-hunger of the thirteenth century, now dropped again to their pre-thirteenth-century level or even lower. On most of the new leases, for which an economic rent was being charged the fines disappeared altogether. So persistent was the fall of values that

---

[2] This and the other references to rural conditions in the fifteenth century are based on the author's forthcoming book on Manorial Profits.

even the value of the demesne farm—and the demesne was frequently farmed with the express purpose of insuring against the fall of agricultural values—declined in the course of years.

Agriculture was thus obviously going through a secular slump, which began at some time in the fourteenth century—in some places before the Black Death—and continued with a slight halt in the first decade or two of the fifteenth century, until the late seventies and the eighties. An agricultural depression so general and continuous in a country as predominantly agricultural as fifteenth-century England would have affected all the other economic activities even if nothing had happened to produce an independent depression in industry and trade. But as it is, we know that independent depression of this kind was taking place in the urban economy as well.

Professor Gras has drawn our attention to the contraction of corn markets. Some such contraction would inevitably have resulted from the decline of agricultural production, but some of it must have resulted from the transformation of the manorial economy and the leasing of the demesne. The establishment of peasant leases on the lands once directly cultivated by the lords has frequently been represented as an "economically progressive" change, the consequence and the cause of the "growing money economy." This conventional view will not stand scrutiny. The large estates of the great secular or episcopal landowners like the Duchy of Lancaster or the Bishop of Winchester used to produce very largely for the market. From the economic point of view large estates of this kind in the late thirteenth century were capitalist concerns: federated grain factories producing largely for cash. The growing of cash crops must have continued after the dissolution of the demesne, for food continued to be bought and sold. But in so far as the peasant holding represented a more self-sufficient type of economy the multiplication of peasant leases represented a tendency towards natural economy and a relative contraction of agricultural exchange.[3]

The diminution of buying and selling in the countryside was in part responsible for the decline of the corporate towns which is another familiar feature of the period. Not all the complaints of the towns at the bad times should be taken at their face value, especially when they were made in order to obtain remission of Royal taxation. Yet, many of the complaints had a foundation of fact. With the exception of London, which continued to grow, of Bristol, which benefited from the resilience of the Western and Southern trades, and possibly of Southampton, which occupied a special position by virtue of its connections with Italian imports and its function as one of the

---

[3] N. S. B. Gras, *The Evolution of the English Corn Market*, pp. 12–44.

outposts of the London region, the bulk of English trading centres, whether the ancient country towns or the old sea-ports, suffered a decline.

In a number of towns, like Norwich, Nottingham, Northampton and Leicester, the decline is shown in the sudden cessation of their territorial expansion. The decay of the older seaports is shown by the fall in their sea-borne trade. It is now well known that the lowest point of English foreign trade was reached at some time in the middle of the century. The ancient Scandinavian connections were repeatedly interrupted in the first half of the century and ceased to count with the definite establishment of the Hanseatic monopoly in Bergen in the second quarter of the century. The Prussian and Polish trade through Danzig was several times blocked in the first half of the century and finally destroyed during the great Anglo-Hanseatic conflict of the mid-century. The local trade of the south coast towns with Picardy, Normandy, and Brittany had succumbed in the early phases of the Hundred Years War, and the ancient and flourishing trade with Gascony was broken by the loss of Aquitaine in the concluding stages of the war. In short, most of the outlying branches of English foreign trade were lopped off, one after another, and by the third quarter of the century the Low Countries remained very nearly the only channel of trade open to the English, and London as the principal centre of that trade was nearly the only great seaport not impoverished by the crisis.[4]

Yet even the trade to the Low Countries, though more active than the other branches of English commerce, did not escape scot-free. Insofar as it was concerned with wool it was bound to be affected by the decline in the wool trade which set in at the second half of the fourteenth century and continued without interruption until it dwindled to a vanishing point in the sixteenth century. We know of course that the dwindling of the wool trade was accompanied and in part compensated by the growth of cloth exports. But we also know now that the compensation was not as full as it was once imagined. The great rise in the English cloth exports occurred in the second half of the fourteenth century. But having grown rapidly and continually for about forty or fifty years the cloth exports and presumably the cloth production then remained stationary throughout most of the fifteenth century and if anything declined in the middle decades. And even at their topmost fifteenth-century level, the cloth exports were not large enough to account for the whole decline of the wool trade.

These facts about cloth must be borne in mind when the so-called

---

[4] E. Power and M. Postan, *English Trade in the Fifteenth Century, passim,* and esp. Professor Gray's essay on "English Foreign Trade from 1446 to 1482."

development of the cloth industry is discussed. That the new industry to some extent made up for the declining income and production elsewhere is undeniable. If the old corporate towns declined, the new cloth-producing villages and towns in East Anglia, Yorkshire and the West Country were springing up, and if old sources of wealth were disappearing new ones were rising in their place. Yet even at its highest the compensation fell short of the deficiency; and over the greater part of the fifteenth century the compensating movements were well below their highest. The flourishing cloth towns did not flourish as abundantly in the fourteen fifties and fourteen sixties as they had done in thirteen eighties and thirteen nineties. And it was not until the last fifteen or twenty years of the century that the fourteenth-century rate of progress was resumed.

The material recession was thus general. To deny its existence or to minimise its extent on the evidence of certain non-material signs is a sin which no economic historian should commit. Even if it is proved that the period was rich in acts of private piety, graced by a flourishing religion, embellished by alabaster statues; better educated, more prettily coiffured and gowned, than any other period in the Middle Ages, the basic facts of material development would still be unaffected. One of the principal tenets of the home-made sociology, which the non-sociological historians commonly assume, is that ages of economic expansion are necessarily ages of intellectual and artistic achievement. As if the generations which make the money also know how to spend it best; and as if the abundance of material means leads inevitably and directly to a corresponding rise in the arts of life.

The pitfalls of this sociology must be remembered when the achievements of the so-called fifteenth-century perpendicular architecture are invoked as evidence of the century's material progress. What do the perpendicular churches prove? Their architectural excellence has nothing to do with either the growth or the decline of English industry, agriculture or trade. Their quantity, the sheer volume of stones and mortar, might be thought to be closely related to economic processes. But were the quantities of stones and mortar shaped in the perpendicular style larger, or even as large as, the stones and mortar that went into the building of the costly parish churches of the twelfth century, the abbeys and the cathedrals of the thirteenth and the fourteenth? And if we, in addition, remember that many of the so-called fifteenth-century buildings were in fact structures, which like King's College Chapel, were commenced at the beginning of the century but not resumed until the coming of the Tudors, or else structures built either before 1425 or after 1475, we shall perhaps be doubly careful in regarding either the cloth villages or their perpendicular churches as evidence of the great commercial efflorescence of the fifteenth century.

But however irrelevant to the period's intellectual and religious activity, the economic recession was certainly consistent with its political situation. The fifteenth century was the time of the last and the most disastrous phase of the Hundred Years War, of misgovernment and civil war at home. The political deterioration began in the closing years of Edward III's reign and was halted for a brief period under the early Lancastrians. But with Henry VI's accession, and especially after his attainment of seniority, the disruption of government led by rapid stages to civil war and military and diplomatic defeats abroad. In things like these a rising tide of production and trade could have been made possible only by a most unusual combination of favourable circumstances: a rapid accumulation of capital, a growth of population, a development of technical arts. The fact that none of these conditions was present makes the economy of the time all the easier to fit into its political background.

II

The redeeming features, such as there were, would be found not in the economic processes but in social relations: not so much on the side of production as on that of distribution. The economic recession was accompanied by social changes some of which may commend themselves to the moral judgment of our own day, even if they do not pass the test of the simple material measurements.

Perhaps the best known were the changes which occurred in the structure and position of the so-called middle classes. With the exception of the families involved in the outlying branches of foreign trade the mercantile elements of English society found themselves in a state of solid conservative prosperity devoid of both the prizes and the penalties of the more adventurous and speculative ages. The great breeding season of English capitalism was in the early phases of the Hundred Years War, the time when the exigencies of Royal finance, new experiments in taxation, speculative ventures with wool, the collapse of Italian finance and the beginning of the new cloth industry, all combined to bring into existence a new race of war financiers and commercial speculators, army purveyors and wool-monopolists. But the race was as short-lived as it was new. The great fortunes were lost as easily as they were made, and the period of reckless finance and gigantic fiscal experiments passed away with the first stage of the war. And while the heroic age of financial adventure was passing away, the speculator and the capitalist found themselves hemmed in by the contracting commercial markets and the slackening tempo of economic development. The Company of the Staple in its final form turned necessity into a policy and organised the wool trade in a way which prevented the development of large single fortunes. And what the Staple did on a national scale the innumerable municipalities and city companies did locally. The English merchant classes responded to the stability and recession of trade in the way of all merchants. They adopted the policy of regulation and restriction, impeding the entry of new recruits into commerce and attempting to share out the available trade. The view of medieval town-economy as one of restrictive and egalitarian monopoly, held and propagated by nineteenth-century historians, largely derives from the municipal and gild documents of the late fourteenth and the fifteenth centuries; and what is sometimes regarded as evidence of a typical medieval regulation is in fact nothing else than instances of fifteenth-century departure from the freer and more speculative conditions of the earlier centuries.

Still better known are the social changes in the villages. The real causes of the agricultural depression still await investigation. But if an anticipatory suggestion may be permitted here it should be pointed out that the most important cause will probably be found in movements of population. The prices of agricultural products, and above all wheat, were depressed, *i.e.* either stationary or gently falling, throughout the period, and the prices naturally affected production. But the action of prices was merely an outward manifestation of other and more fundamental processes. It was both caused and accompanied by a decline of the agricultural population of which there are innumerable signs.

The effect of a falling population and depressed prices on the condition of the peasants is easily imagined. It meant a greater supply of land and lower rents. The great overcrowding and land-hunger of the thirteenth century gave place to an oversupplied land market: there were fewer small-holders, and the full peasant holdings were on the whole held on more favourable conditions, sometimes at a lower rent, and nearly always free of labour services.

The improvement in the position of the landholder was accompanied by an improvement in the position of the hired labourer. With the decline in the numbers of the small-holding population the wages of agricultural labour rose. But while they were rising, prices remained either stationary or declined, and hence the "golden age of the English agricultural labourer" which Rogers discovered in the fifteenth century.

The real sufferers from the agricultural depression were therefore the landlords. The depression of prices and the rising costs of labour made the cultivation of the demesne unprofitable; the revenue from rents which at first grew with the letting out of the demesne was in

137

the end affected by the "vacancies" and the general fall of agricultural values. In short, in the countryside the main burden of economic change was borne by the upper ranks of society.

How far their dwindling revenue contributed to their restlessness and prompted them to seek additional income in political gangsterdom of the times we shall never know for certain. We can only surmise that in an age of dwindling agricultural profits seigneurial revenues derived from feudal rights and privileges were all the more valuable and all the more worth fighting for. And if attempts to defend and increase the feudal hold over local offices and revenues is to be discerned behind the personal struggles of baronial parties, then the agricultural depression can be said to have contributed, albeit indirectly, to that great reconstruction of the English landowning classes which prepared and maintained the rule of the Tudors. It is in this sense, more than in any other, that the roots of the sixteenth century will be found in the fifteenth.

Some Suggested Readings

Carus-Wilson, Eleanor M. "Evidences of Industrial Growth on Some Fifteenth-Century Manors," *The Economic History Review*, XII (1959), 190–205.

Cipolla, Carlo M., Lopez, Robert S., Miskimin, Harry A. "Economic Depression of the Renaissance?" *The Economic History Review*, XVI (1964), 519–24.

Helleiner, Karl F. "Population Movement and Agrarian Depression in the Later Middle Ages," *Canadian Journal of Economics and Political Science*, XV (1949), 368–77.

Lopez, R. S. and Miskimin, Harry A. "The Economic Depression of the Renaissance," *The Economic History Review*, XIV (1962), 408–26.

Postan, Michael M. "Some Economic Evidence of Declining Population in the Later Middle Ages," *The Economic History Review*, II (1950), 221–46.

Turner, Ralph E. "Economic Discontent in Medieval Western Europe," *Journal of Economic History, Supplement*, VIII (1948), 85–100.